The Home Chef's
SOUS VIDE COOKBOOK

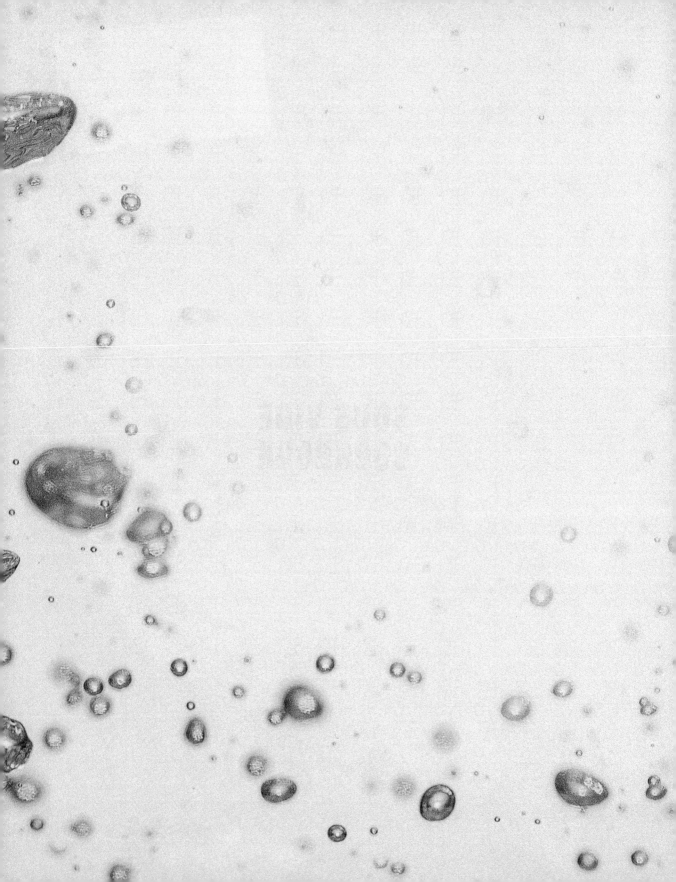

The Home Chef's
SOUS VIDE COOKBOOK

Elevated Recipes for Your Favorite Meats and Sides

by Jenna Passaro

Photography by Alicia Cho

ROCKRIDGE PRESS

For general information on our other products and services or to obtain technical support, please contact our Customer Care Department within the United States at (866) 744-2665, or outside the United States at (510) 253-0500.

Rockridge Press publishes its books in a variety of electronic and print formats. Some content that appears in print may not be available in electronic books, and vice versa.

TRADEMARKS: Rockridge Press and the Rockridge Press logo are trademarks or registered trademarks of Callisto Media Inc. and/or its affiliates, in the United States and other countries, and may not be used without written permission. All other trademarks are the property of their respective owners. Rockridge Press is not associated with any product or vendor mentioned in this book.

Interior and Cover Designer: Heather Krakora
Art Producer: Michael Hardgrove
Editor: Michael Goodman
Production Editor: Matthew Burnett

Photography © 2019 Alicia Cho.
Food styling by Ashley Nevarez.
Illustrations © Tom Bingham.
Background © iStockphoto.com.
Author photograph: Eloquent Moments Photography

ISBN: Print 978-1-646-11129-9
       eBook 978-1-646-11130-5

R0

*To Patrick, my partner in life and the kitchen.
And to Baby G., whose first taste of beef was sous vide
Denver steak and who inspires me every day to make
food he won't throw on the ground.*

CONTENTS

INTRODUCTION

I grew up making such a mess in the kitchen that I was banned from using it for a while.

And even though I'm now grown, with my own kitchen, I'm still making a mess experimenting with different ingredients, flavors, and tools. A day without getting creative in the kitchen feels like an empty day.

My quest to cook amazing things in the kitchen was sparked in 2015 when I met the love of my life. As fate would have it, he was a cook at my favorite place to eat in town, a James Beard Award–winning restaurant. I learned so much from him, particularly about confidence, taking risks, and embracing the idea that the smoke detector going off is nothing but a sign that a delicious meal is almost ready. Probably the most eye-opening realization from our early days cooking together in my tiny little kitchen was that restaurant-quality meals can be made at home.

Becoming engaged was not only the preview of our married life together, but it also began our very steady relationship with sous vide cooking at home. Before then, Patrick, my soon-to-be husband, had experience with precision cooking in restaurant kitchens, but sous vide cooking wasn't widely available to home chefs.

So, like many home chefs, our sous vide machine found us. Patrick left the restaurant world and began working for a tech startup. His boss, who was a total foodie, gave us a sous vide machine as a present. He swore by this newly available kitchen tool. But, to be honest, we didn't really know what the heck to do with it.

I was intrigued by the sous vide machine, but I also was overwhelmed. At the time, there wasn't much information out there for home chefs to learn how to cook amazing meals with precision cookers. I had heard we could make the most delicious steaks of our lives but was confused by limited and conflicting advice on cooking times, temperatures, preparation techniques, and finishing touch recommendations.

After moving to Portland, I began a recipe and travel site for foodies, Sip Bite Go, which inspired me to dive into learning how I could best use sous vide machines for everyday cooking.

Patrick and I tried every cut of meat we could find: rib-eye, pork loin, turkey legs, filet—then we started to try vegetables. If I liked it, I tried to sous vide it! We spent many nights up until three in the morning, drinking wine and getting the perfect sear on a hunk of brisket that wouldn't be ready for another 36 hours.

I loved the anticipation, the smell of the sous vide bath filling our home with fragrant rosemary and garlic or whatever seasonings we experimented with that day. It was such a reward when the time came to cut into the vacuum-sealed bag of meat to discover what intense flavors awaited.

Fast forward to today: We are married with a baby! We still cook most nights at home, but we are more efficient with meal planning, as well as the time we spend in the kitchen. Along the way, I've meticulously recorded a ton of sous vide recipes that fit our lifestyle, from preparing Buffalo-style sous vide chicken wings for football parties, to prepping a juicy sous vide New York strip for dinner.

While we still take the time for short ribs and larger cuts of meat, being a young family means taking kitchen shortcuts. So, I'm often prepping and cooking sous vide recipes in the morning, then refrigerating them until it's time for a fast and easy sear, broil, or grill to fix dinner.

Now that our baby is eating solids and goes to bed early, we don't do a lot of eating out at restaurants. I'm so thankful that sous vide lets us feel like our normal, pre-baby selves by making it possible for us to enjoy luxurious, restaurant-quality meals at home.

I can't wait to share my family's recipes so you can also eat well at home.

Let's dig in!

CHAPTER

ONE

find recipe on page 65

TIME
WILL
TELL

I want to help you create meals based on the most helpful and delicious qualities of sous vide cooking. This book is intended for all levels of home chefs and all levels of experience with sous vide.

Newbies, I want to inspire you to take out your sous vide machine and use it regularly to treat yourself to restaurant-quality meals at home. Use this book as your guide to learn which cuts of meat and vegetables are the best to cook sous vide style and how to prepare them.

Experienced sous vide home chefs, I want to help you build your skillset. This means pushing you beyond just making a sous vide steak, to teaching you how to orchestrate an entire meal. It means getting a firm grasp on flavors and sauces that will complement your sous vide cooking, learning excellent wine pairings, and using the plating tips to make your meals shine. In addition, you'll learn meal-planning tips, easy recipes to entertain and impress guests, and how to use sous vide leftovers.

WORTH THE WAIT

Sous vide machines regulate the heat of water so that food is cooked at a consistent temperature. With this method of cooking, home chefs have more control over the texture and taste of the food being prepared. Steak, chicken, and pork are impossible to overcook when using a sous vide machine, whereas cooking these foods on the stove, grill, or in the oven can be a complete guessing game, even with a thermometer.

Sous vide cooking allows you to prepare food in a way you haven't been able to before. One of the first recipes I got excited about was poached eggs, which are ridiculously labor-intensive when made the traditional way on the stove. The sous vide machine makes the most perfect poached eggs that turn out creamy and delicious every time.

You may have heard people rave about sous vide's "edge-to-edge cooking." When you cook a steak on a traditional hot surface, such as a grill, the center of the steak may be a perfect medium-rare, but up to a half-inch of the edges will be more well done. But with sous vide, the steak cooks evenly from edge to edge—the entire piece is a perfect medium-rare, or medium, as desired.

MEAL PLANNING JUST GOT EASIER

With sous vide cooking, you can prep and season meals in bulk and freeze them in airtight plastic bags for when you want them. As busy new parents, this has been a lifesaver for us. Prepping frozen sous vide bags is a great option for when I know I'm going to have a busy week and won't have the time to spend hours in the kitchen.

For many sous vide recipes, all you need is additional cooking time—the general rule of thumb for a frozen steak is to just add another 60 minutes, which isn't that long to wait for a perfectly cooked piece of meat.

Due to the pasteurization process that occurs in sous vide cooking, your food's shelf life is extended. This is an essential part of sous vide science to know because food safety temperatures are a bit different when using the sous vide method of cooking. Cooking food at lower temperatures still meets food safety standards because the longer cooking time kills bacteria and results in safely pasteurized food.

When cooking sous vide style, you are easily able to reheat your meat or finish it for serving. You can cook the meat in the sous vide bath, then save the final step of searing, grilling, broiling, or torching (which only takes 5 to 10 minutes) for when you are ready to eat.

Another valuable component is that you can prepare food further in advance, and with tastier results, than traditional methods of cooking. Sous vide food will taste great for 5 to 7 days. That means you can sous vide a week's worth of steaks on a Sunday and enjoy them with minimal time in the kitchen for days to come. I frequently use pre-prepped sous vide food in salads, tacos, quesadillas, egg scrambles, pasta dishes, and rice bowls.

Sous vide cooking for everyday use means never eating cold or taste-less reheated food again. If you have family members coming home at different times, they can each pop their food in a pan to sear or in the oven to crisp for just a few minutes.

Sous vide also prevents food waste caused by food burning or becoming dry. And despite the longer cooking times, I have found that it does not hike up my electricity bill. Sous vide allows me to easily cook meals well in advance and prevents us from running out of time to cook and subsequently resorting to subpar takeout food.

PARTY TIME

This kitchen tool is a party hit. Sous vide is extremely versatile, which is why it's fun to incorporate sous vide recipes when entertaining guests.

For some hosts, a dinner party can be very intimidating because you need to focus on both socializing and preparing a memorable meal. With sous vide, you can cook the appetizers the day before and then finish them off a few minutes before the event. For example, we host a lot of football game events, and my sous vide chicken wings are always a hit. I sous vide the wings the day before or the morning of the game. And when people start to arrive for the game, I toss the wings under the broiler with Buffalo sauce for a few minutes. Everyone raves how tender and juicy the wings are, and they are completely unaware of how easy they were to prepare and how I was able to do so ahead of time.

While other methods of slow-cooking meat exist to achieve a tender texture, many of them are more labor-intensive and aren't a wise choice for premium (read: expensive) cuts of meat. With sous vide, you can trust that your meal is cooking to perfection even when you're busy entertaining family and friends.

For more formal dinner hosting events, or even "date nights in," we often choose pork or steak to get that restaurant-quality meal at home, and we don't have to worry about precise timing. Sous vide cooking is pretty flexible; steaks, for example, can cook anywhere between 1 to 4 hours. That way, if your dinner guests run late, or something else comes up, it's no big deal if you can't take the food out of the water bath right away. Ten minutes before I expect to serve the meal, the steaks get a quick sear, and again, no one knows how easy it was to make and prepare the perfect meal.

SAFE SCIENCE

But—plastic? Can that be safe? If you're wondering about cooking with heated plastic and at lower temperatures than you're used to with traditional cooking, I understand your concerns. When I was pregnant, I was naturally very concerned about food safety and researched it carefully. The guidelines tell us to buy heat-safe plastic zip-top bags that have been tested for sous vide use. I would suggest that you not use anything that's not approved for sous vide (or high temperature) cooking. Also, make sure not to use the bags for any longer than they are guaranteed safe or approved for use.

A natural alternative to cooking in plastic is using mason jars, but they aren't appropriate for the majority of dishes due to size limitations and techniques. Mason jars are best for pickling and some recipes using eggs that won't be shocked in an ice bath after cooking. The jars may crack from the temperature change.

There are some reusable silicone bags available on the market that may be a good alternative if you're looking to explore options beyond vacuum seal and plastic zip-top bags.

Another thing that concerned me when I was pregnant was the safety of some food temperatures recommended for cooking sous vide, compared to how I normally prepared food. I was reassured to learn that the longer cook time still kills harmful bacteria—even at the lower temperatures for sous vide foods.

OUT OF THE LAB, INTO THE KITCHEN

Did You Know: The term "sous vide" is French for "under vacuum."

Sous vide techniques began as safety measures to pasteurize and sterilize food for hospitals, labs, and large food companies. In 1974, the science of sous vide was exposed to the restaurant scene. French chef Georges Pralus used the new method to solve an unlikely challenge: Finding a new way to cook foie gras that resulted in the least amount of fat being lost in the process. To the surprise of many, sous vide was the cooking method that not only retained the most fat in the foie gras but also retained the best flavor. No one could believe the dish was the result of food cooked in plastic in a water bath.

For a couple of decades, sous vide cooking was limited to professional kitchens due to cost. A proper sous vide setup cost upward of a thousand dollars. However, to the delight of creative home chefs everywhere, in 2009, lower-priced immersion circulators debuted. Today, there are more than 100 options available.

EQUIPMENT NEEDS

The magic of sous vide comes from submerging food in precise, temperature-controlled water that conducts heat far better than the air that fills your oven.

When you set the sous vide temperature at 140°F, the water bath will reach that temperature, and so will the innermost portion of the food—and it will stay at that temperature for as long as you need it. This precision—the ability to completely control both temperature and time—is what leads to the wonderful results that sous vide cooking provides for home chefs. As such, it is important that you have the correct equipment and supplies to safely and most effectively conduct this type of food preparation. I know from personal experience that learning a new style of food prep and choosing kitchen supplies and equipment can be a bit overwhelming. It is my hope that you will find what you need within this book to alleviate your worries and help you make informed decisions to support your new adventure in the kitchen.

First, let's discuss some absolute necessities for sous vide cooking. Then we can move on to some items that are not absolutely necessary but nice to have.

Please keep in mind that these are my personal suggestions, based on more than a fair amount of experience. However, I recognize that there are other opinions and preferences out there. Feel free to do your homework, but I'm confident that you'll be happy with the options and suggestions listed here.

MUST HAVE

Sous vide machine. There are two types of devices to consider.

- The first is an all-in-one **combination container and circulator**. This is a smaller-scale version of what you'll find in many restaurants.

- The other type of device used by many home cooks is a practical and space-conscious **immersion circulator** that you attach to a **bath container** (such as a kitchen bucket or stockpot) that holds water (see Circulator Choices, page 9).

Sous vide container. My favorite containers are large, deep stockpots and clear professional kitchen-grade containers. I recommend starting with one that will hold at least 12 quarts (liters). Clear sides let you see how the water is circulating around the food and make it easy to check the water level.

Food storage containers/bags. This is another area where you have several options to consider.

- **Vacuum sealer bags or heat-safe freezer bags.** These are the most popular way to hold food submerged in the sous vide bath. A vacuum sealer is preferred for home chefs who will be sous vide cooking regularly, as it provides the most leak-proof option. Freezer bags are sometimes harder to use when trying to properly place food in a flat layer. For instance, if you sous vide Brussels sprouts or chicken wings, the ingredients need to be in a flat layer within the bag in order to cook evenly and in the time dictated by the recipe. Getting them in a flat layer is easier to do with a vacuum sealer on a flat surface. Plus, it's really fun to watch food vacuum seal! Vacuum sealers start at about $99. They also make it easy to meal prep and freeze sous vide recipes in advance.

- **Reusable silicone bags.** There are reusable bags and kits on the market that can help remove the air from bags. These may be your preference if you're reluctant to buy an additional kitchen gadget and don't want to create plastic waste.

- **Mason jars.** These are wonderful, but not for all recipes, partly because you can't vacuum seal them in quite the same way. For instance, I wouldn't sous vide shrimp or chicken in a mason jar. But I do like to keep a stash of various size mason jars on hand for pickling and for specialty recipes such as egg bites (page 20).

Cast iron skillet. After the sous vide machine, the number-one tool I'd recommend for home chefs is a 10- to 12-inch cast iron skillet. This may seem counterintuitive—isn't the whole idea behind sous vide dispensing with high heat? But the fact is that some foods, particularly meat, just don't look very appetizing when they come out of the bath. The inside has cooked to a perfect internal temperature, but the outside needs a good sear to appeal to both the eyes and the belly. A quick 2 to 3 minutes in a cast iron skillet on high heat will make food fresh from the sous vide bath instantly become restaurant-quality in both taste and appearance. A good cast iron skillet will sear the surface to create that beautifully browned look, add a little bit of crunchy texture, and lock in all the flavor. High heat is absolutely essential to sear without overcooking, and inexpensive lightweight frying pans just won't cut it; you won't regret investing in a high-quality cast iron skillet.

There are other ways to finish sous vide food, and it's fun to experiment—I encourage you to try them all. Get sexy grill marks on steaks and lobster tails with the help of an outdoor grill, Searzall, or another type of torch. And for indoor cooking, try finishing off recipes with a quick broil or a few minutes in the air fryer.

NICE TO HAVE

Vacuum sealer. When I'm working with premium ingredients, I want to be sure they cook perfectly, and a vacuum sealer reduces the risk of leaks or water getting into the food.

Torch. These can be fun! They can also be quite dangerous. But it's only a matter of time before most sous vide enthusiasts want to dabble with a final step of direct fire, so having a torch on hand that you know how to use safely is a great way to give your meat a quick sear before serving.

Lids. These are a great way to maintain a safe and effective water level in the sous vide bath. They are especially handy to minimize evaporation for long cooking times over 4 hours. You can either buy a lid and cut out a corner for the immersion circulator, or you can opt for a lid that is precut to fit your sous vide machine. Some people use aluminum foil or plastic wrap for a similar result. There are also small insulated balls available to purchase that claim to lock in the heat. I even know someone who uses kids' play pit balls to insulate their sous vide baths. I don't recommend that, but my point is that there's a lot of room to DIY a sous vide rig.

CIRCULATOR CHOICES

There is a wide variety of sous vide cooking devices on the market, which can be intimidating to first-time buyers or those looking for an upgrade.

What should you look for when purchasing your circulator? It depends on your budget, and decent circulators can be found for as little as $60 or $70. However, remember that price does not always determine the quality of the device. That's where the specs come in.

Read product reviews to be aware how accurate the device is at maintaining the right temperature. A consistent temperature is the key to sous vide cooking.

As with any heat source, sous vide cooking devices take time to warm up. So, a device that warms the water speedily is worth considering. An effective device should only take about 15 minutes.

Some devices come with Wi-Fi and Bluetooth capability, often with accompanying apps, that you may find convenient in using to control your device from afar.

Weights and clips. Some foods naturally rise to the top and float in the sous vide bath. This means that water won't properly circulate around the food, resulting in uneven cooking. Food grade weights the size of marbles are available to hold down the sous vide bag. Sometimes clips can also be used on the side of the sous vide container to help hold down the food.

Weighted rack divider. This tool is another way to properly place food in the sous vide bath. It comes in handy when cooking for a large event or doing meal prep for the week. The packs of sealed food are placed in columns, allowing the water to flow around the food evenly for precise cooking.

Cutting board. I recommend always placing a cutting board under the sous vide bath. Some people have had the misfortune of cracking natural stone countertops from the heat of the sous vide bath, so using a cutting board is a great precaution to take.

SOUS VIDE IN THREE STEPS

There are three main steps when preparing your meal sous vide style. The first step is seasoning the food and sealing the bag with as little air as possible. The second step is the cooking process, which requires dropping the bag of food into a water bath set to temperature by the circulator for a set time. And the final step is the finishing touch, when the food is seared, grilled, broiled, or air fried for a stunning look and additional boost of flavor.

VACUUM VERSUS FREEZER BAG

The easiest and most common way to prepare food for your circulator is with a vacuum sealer, which completely removes the air and makes it easier to prevent your food from floating in the sous vide bath. However, a heat-safe freezer bag can also do the trick if you don't want the additional expense of a vacuum sealer.

One common trick to getting the air out of the freezer bag is the water displacement method. To do this, seal the bag almost all the way. Slowly submerge the bag in water while keeping the opening of the bag out of the water. As the bag is pushed down, the water pressure will push the air out of the bag. Assist the air escaping the bag until there is no air left. Then seal the bag.

One thing to keep in mind is that freezer bags aren't ideal for all cooking temperatures. At higher temperatures, the seams can fail, which means the food will get wet and lose flavor to the water bath. Consult the recipes and instructions on the bags to make sure they are only used for dishes cooking at temperatures appropriate for the bags.

UNDER WATER

Cooking sous vide style is a pretty hands-off process once the food is submerged. Since the internal temperature of the food will never rise above the temperature of the water, you don't need to stand by and watch the food cook. Check to make sure the water level remains plentiful and the food is not floating. The sous vide machine does the rest!

THE FINISH: PAN, GRILL, OR TORCH?

This final step is my favorite (well, outside of watching the food get vacuum sealed). In just a few minutes under an intense heat source—the grill, torch, broiler, air fryer, etc.—the food will have the desired look and taste to rival your favorite restaurants.

For most foods, any of the aforementioned finishing methods will work. For a busy weeknight, I usually toss meat or seafood on the grill or in a cast iron skillet on medium-high "better turn on the fan" heat. Cast iron skillets work better than regular pans because they are able to retain a high heat and have a texture that cooks food just right.

The broiler is another favorite way I finish sous vide food. I love using it for chicken, fish, ribs, and veggies. I'll usually add a barbecue sauce and give the food a quick broil on high.

TIPS & TROUBLESHOOTING FAQ

It's easy to get the hang of sous vide cooking, but there can be a learning curve for the at-home chef. New sous vide users aren't always clear on certain steps and best practices. And some aspects can be a bit tricky at first. Here are some common questions for both first-time and intermediate sous vide cooks.

When should I season food?

In general, the best time to season your meat is right before you seal the food in the bag. This ensures that while the food is cooking it absorbs all the flavors.

However, as this type of cooking evolves, there's been some debate in the sous vide enthusiast community over which types of seasonings should be added before the sous vide bath and which seasonings should be added in the final step (in the cast iron skillet, grill, etc.).

Most of my recipes call for using aromatics and salt before the sous vide bath. I'll often experiment with different flavored salts (e.g., barbecue salt, smoked salt), and various herbs. And I always throw in some garlic or shallots. We just can't get enough garlic in my house!

The final step, when the food is finished on the grill or in a cast iron skillet, is a great time to add spices and other flavors. And I always save some herbs to sprinkle on the food at the end.

Do you need to marinate meat before sous vide cooking?

I've enjoyed many sous vide dishes where I marinate the meat before putting it in the bag. However, using a vacuum sealer with liquid can be tricky, so lately I've moved away from that.

Do you add butter or oil to the bag?

This has become another hot debate among sous vide cooks. In the early days, I would always sous vide meat and seafood with a chunk of butter or olive oil. The latest trend is to skip adding these fats, as it is thought to cause the tasty juices to leach out of the meat. I no longer add butter and oil to most of my sous vide recipes because it may dilute the flavor of the meat or change the texture. To be safe, if you would like to include oil or butter in your recipe, I suggest in most cases that you add it during the searing/broiling process.

Can I salt before storing or freezing?

Definitely. One of the best things about sous vide is that you can cook your food from frozen. Add salt and any other herbs or spices you desire, then bag and freeze it.

What happens when I leave something cooking longer than recommended? Do I throw it out?

You'll find that many recipes are accommodating to various durations of cooking. For example, I know I can throw steak in the sous vide bath, and it will have a predictable taste and texture for 1 to 4 hours of cook time. This is helpful to know but can be confusing for new sous vide home chefs. When you do leave your meat to cook beyond the window of cook time recommended, you may find that it has become soggy. It's still safe to eat, but you may not find the texture very pleasant.

Does pre-searing make sense?

For the majority of recipes, searing before sous vide is thought to have little to no effect. Some people claim it does not change the taste or texture significantly and is not necessary. However, there are some foods I like to pre-sear. A large piece of meat, such as a 3-pound pork shoulder, is a good example. Similar to how I'd cook it in a crockpot, I sear this type of meat with the flavors I want, then sous vide it. When it comes out of the sous vide bath after a long overnight cook, it's falling apart and ready to shred.

Can I chill and reheat food after cooking sous vide style if I haven't opened the bag?

Yes. Once the food is cooked, chill it right away. Ideally, you'll shock it in an ice bath first. You can then do the final step of finishing the meat in a cast iron skillet or grill. This is a great idea for meal prep.

Can I cook bagged food straight from the freezer?

Absolutely. This is one of my favorite sous vide cooking tricks. There have been so many nights I've been falling asleep in bed only to realize I didn't move meat to be defrosted for dinner the next night. Once I remember I can sous vide the frozen meat directly from the freezer, just adding about an hour of extra cook time, I can fall fast asleep.

ABOUT THE RECIPES

My collections of sous vide recipes focus on cooking easy-to-find proteins and vegetables that offer the biggest advantages when using the sous vide method. My husband, friends, and family have been very loyal taste-testers throughout the years as I've explored the best ingredients to match the true potential of sous vide cooking. I've meticulously fiddled with various times and temperatures in order to find a favorite for each item I sous vide.

The recipes in this book are the ones I am most fond of cooking sous vide style. I encourage you to get creative in your kitchen, testing new versions of these recipes to suit your own tastes. Along the way I've included alternative ingredient suggestions to help get those creative juices flowing.

When starting out on the sous vide cooking journey, most people stick to making one ingredient at a time: a steak, a chicken breast, a pork roast. This makes sense when you're trying to master the sous vide technique, but it can be easy to ignore the sides and sauces that round out the meal. My goal is to help you turn sous vide foods into whole dishes. You'll find recommendations for toppings and servings that will help you create wonderfully complete plated meals.

Let's get started!

CHAPTER TWO

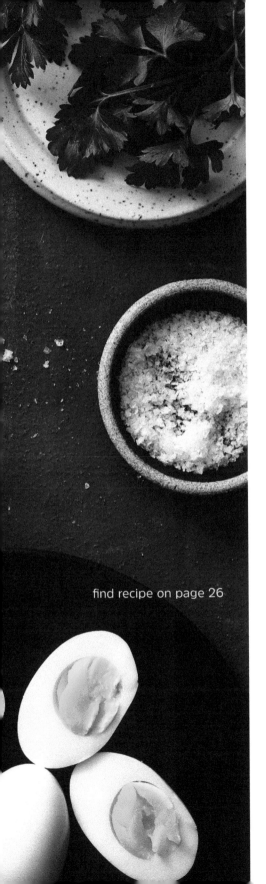

find recipe on page 26

EGGS

Cooking eggs sous vide style opens up a world of breakfast and brunch options to home chefs. There was a time when I would eat poached eggs only when I was out for brunch. Now, I can make them perfectly any morning in my own kitchen.

Mornings are so easy when egg dishes are prepared in advance. Avocado toast can quickly be assembled on a busy workday morning from eggs already soft boiled with the sous vide machine. There's no way to overcook them, unlike when you use traditional methods of boiling eggs in a pot of water on the stove. Once you learn the basics of eggs cooked sous vide, it's time to move on to the fancy side of sous vide eggs, including those wonderful sous vide egg cups made in mason jars—and even French toast. There are plenty of recipes here to help you begin your day inspired.

EGGS

BACON, CARAMELIZED ONION, AND CHEESE EGG BITES

Serves 6   Prep time: 25 minutes | Cook time: 1 hour, 30 minutes | Finishing time: 5 minutes

Sous vide egg bites are all the rage—and for good reason! Making egg bites with the precision cooker produces soft, fluffy, creamy, and souffle-like eggs with minimal effort. These egg bites are so versatile, you can easily adapt this recipe to include your favorite ingredients. I love making these for overnight guests because they are simple to make ahead of time, and they taste just like the coffee-chain version that is currently all the rage. This recipe uses six 4-ounce mason jars to hold the eggs in the sous vide bath.

1½ tablespoons olive oil, divided

1 medium red onion, thinly sliced

6 bacon slices

5 large eggs

¼ cup 2% milk

¼ cup shredded fontina cheese

¼ teaspoon salt

¼ teaspoon freshly ground black pepper

Olive oil cooking spray

1 tablespoon finely chopped fresh cilantro (optional)

1. Preheat the sous vide bath to 172°F.

2. In a small sauté pan or skillet over medium heat, heat 1 tablespoon of olive oil. Add the onion and cook, stirring regularly so the onions don't burn, for 10 minutes. Reduce the heat to medium-low, add the remaining ½ tablespoon of olive oil, and continue stirring regularly until the onions are completely soft and brown, 5 to 10 minutes more. If the onions begin to burn at any time, add 1 to 2 tablespoons of water. Once done, remove them from the heat and set aside.

3. In a medium frying pan over medium heat, cook the bacon for 5 to 8 minutes on each side until browned. Remove from the heat and lay the slices on a paper towel–lined plate. Once cooled, dice the bacon and set aside.

4. In a large bowl, scramble the eggs. Whisk in the milk, fontina cheese, salt, and pepper. Transfer the egg mixture to a measuring cup with a spout and set aside.

5. Spray six 4-ounce mason jars with cooking spray. Fill the jars two-thirds full with the prepared egg mixture. Add the cooked bacon and caramelized onions. Seal the jars tightly.

6. Sous vide the egg bites for 1 hour. Once done, carefully remove the jars from the water bath. The egg bites should be set and not runny. To eat immediately, run a knife along the outside of the egg bites to pop them out of the mason jars.

7. To finish, plate and top with the cilantro (if using).

8. To store the egg bites for later, let the jars cool on the counter for 15 to 20 minutes until cool to the touch, then refrigerate them for up to 1 week.

PREP TIP Make a batch of these to enjoy an easy breakfast during the week. Reheat them in the microwave for 15 to 30 seconds.

POACHED EGGS ON ROASTED TOMATOES

Serves 4   Prep time: 10 minutes | Cook time: 1 hour | Finishing time: 20 minutes

Poached eggs were one of the first sous vide recipes I mastered. Since English muffins are the norm, I wanted to use something else to make them special when we had overnight guests. I quickly came to love how easy and beautiful it is to serve poached eggs on roasted tomatoes. The tomatoes take about the same time to cook as the eggs, but they cook in the oven, making them relatively hands-off after a couple minutes of prep. Poaching eggs isn't too hard, either, since the eggs are dropped into the water bath while still in their shell. This dish is perfect when paired with hollandaise sauce.

FOR THE ROASTED TOMATOES

1½ tablespoons minced garlic

1 tablespoon olive oil

1 tablespoon red wine vinegar

Salt

Freshly ground black pepper

4 beefsteak tomatoes

FOR THE EGGS

8 large eggs

Salt

Freshly ground black pepper

1 tablespoon chopped fresh parsley

1 tablespoon chopped fresh chives (optional)

1 recipe Hollandaise Sauce (page 160)

Smoked paprika

TO PREPARE THE TOMATOES

1. Preheat the oven to 300°F. Line a rimmed baking sheet with parchment paper.
2. In a medium mixing bowl, combine the garlic, olive oil, red wine vinegar, salt, and pepper.
3. Slice the tomatoes in half horizontally and arrange on the prepared baking sheet. Drizzle the olive oil mixture on top of the tomatoes. Roast for 1 hour or until the tomatoes are soft and slightly charred.

TO PREPARE THE EGGS

1. While the tomatoes are roasting, preheat the sous vide machine to 145°F.
2. Carefully place the eggs (in their shells) on the bottom of the machine and sous vide for 45 minutes. In the last few minutes of cooking time, bring a small pot of water to a slow rolling boil on the stovetop (this will be used to finish the poached eggs).
3. While the eggs are cooking, prepare the hollandaise sauce.

4. Once cooked, carefully remove the poached eggs from the water bath. Crack an egg carefully into a bowl. You'll notice a soft jiggly yolk surrounded by a thin layer of egg white. Stir the boiling water in the pot in a circle before lowering the egg into the water; this will help the egg white wrap around the yolk once it's in the pot. Use a slotted spoon to gently lower the egg from the bowl into the boiling water. Let it rest in the boiling water for 1 minute. Discard any excess egg white that is not attached to the egg.

5. After 1 minute, or when the egg white is cooked, remove the egg and place it on a paper towel–lined plate to catch any runoff water. Repeat with each egg until they are all poached. To work quickly, you can use multiple pots of boiling water or do multiple eggs at a time.

6. To finish, place the poached eggs on top of the roasted tomatoes and top with hollandaise sauce. Season with a pinch of smoked paprika per egg and a sprinkle of salt and pepper. Garnish with the parsley and chives, if using.

MAKE-AHEAD TIP The roasted tomatoes can be made a day in advance and reheated for 10 minutes in the oven before serving.

BOILED EGG SALAD SANDWICH

Serves 4   Prep time: 5 minutes | Cook time: 40 minutes | Finishing time: 15 minutes

Sous vide lets you whip up easy egg salad sandwiches. The eggs turn out firm with creamy yolks. This recipe is an easy one to meal prep for the week. In addition to making killer sandwiches, leftover boiled eggs can be used in a variety of other dishes. We came to love this recipe for taking on mini road trips around the Pacific Northwest.

8 large eggs

4 bacon slices, cooked and crumbled (optional)

2 tablespoons diced red onion

1 tablespoon chopped fresh chives

¼ cup Greek yogurt

½ teaspoon Dijon mustard

¼ teaspoon smoked paprika

¼ teaspoon salt

¼ teaspoon freshly ground black pepper

4 sesame rolls

1. Preheat the sous vide machine to 150°F.

2. Carefully place the eggs (in their shells) on the bottom of the machine and sous vide for 40 minutes. When done, transfer the eggs to an ice bath for 5 minutes to stop the cooking process.

3. To finish, peel and chop the eggs.

4. In a large mixing bowl, gently combine the eggs, bacon (if using), red onion, and chives. Set aside.

5. In a small mixing bowl, whisk together the Greek yogurt, Dijon mustard, smoked paprika, salt, and pepper. Fold the sauce into the egg mixture.

6. Spoon the egg salad onto sesame rolls and enjoy within 2 days.

SUBSTITUTION TIP Swap in the same amount of mayonnaise for Greek yogurt for a more traditional egg salad sandwich.

SCRAMBLED EGGS

Serves 4   Prep time: 10 minutes | Cook time: 20 minutes | Finishing time: 5 minutes

Using sous vide for scrambled eggs is a little more hands-on than other dishes, but it's also very fast. I make my scramble with the same ingredients my grandma used, including a dash of milk. When making scrambled eggs for a leisurely weekend brunch, I serve them with a side of chorizo or Italian sausage and hash browns. Even if you have a vacuum sealer, I recommend using the water displacement technique with a zip-top bag for this recipe. Plus, you'll need some clips or weights to help hold down the eggs.

8 large eggs

1 tablespoon 2% milk

¼ teaspoon salt

¼ teaspoon freshly ground black pepper

1 tablespoon finely chopped fresh chives

1. Preheat the sous vide machine to 165°F.

2. In a medium mixing bowl, whisk together the eggs, milk, salt, and pepper. Pour the egg mixture into a plastic zip-top bag and leave the bag open.

3. When the water bath is ready, use the water displacement method (see page 10) to gently lower the eggs into the water while releasing as much air as possible from the bag. Once the air is out, the bag is sealed, and the eggs are fully submerged, use clips or weights to keep the eggs submerged while keeping the bag in a position for easy removal from the water.

4. Sous vide in 5-minute intervals, for a total of 15 minutes. Remove the bag every 5 minutes to massage the bag of eggs with kitchen towel–lined hands for 30 seconds. The total time to create scrambled eggs, including cooking and massaging, will be about 17 minutes.

5. To finish, remove the eggs from the sous vide bath once complete and serve garnished with the chives.

PREP TIP The perfect texture for scrambled eggs is fluffy, not runny. If the eggs are still runny, add an additional 1 to 2 minutes of cook time.

SOFTBOILED EGG AVOCADO TOAST

Serves 4   Prep time: 5 minutes | Cook time: 10 minutes | Finishing time: 5 minutes

Softboiled eggs make it easy to enjoy sous vide cooked eggs in a variety of popular dishes, including one that is super popular in Portland, Oregon: avocado toast. The bright, cheery yellow yolks stand out against white serving platters, and if you're serving these for brunch, guests can choose to add a variety of other ingredients, such as hot sauce, everything bagel seasoning, tomatoes, or corn.

4 large eggs

2 avocados, pitted
  and mashed

4 slices toast

Salt

Freshly ground
  black pepper

Hot sauce (optional)

1 tablespoon chopped
  fresh parsley

1. Preheat the sous vide machine to 194°F.

2. Carefully place the eggs (in their shells) in the bottom of the machine and sous vide for 9 minutes. When done, transfer the eggs to an ice bath for 5 minutes to stop the cooking process. Peel the eggs and slice in half or leave whole for plating. Set aside.

3. To finish, spread some mashed avocado on each piece of toast and top with 1 egg. Add a sprinkle of salt and pepper, plus a dash of hot sauce (if using). Garnish with the parsley.

SUBSTITUTION TIP Use a sprinkle of red pepper flakes in place of the hot sauce, if desired.

FRENCH TOAST WITH CANDIED PECANS

Serves 4 | Prep time: 10 minutes | Cook time: 1 hour, 30 minutes | Finishing time: 10 minutes

This French toast is one of my favorite sous vide–style brunch dishes—you'll love it for entertaining. I found that a thick, dense bread, such as brioche, holds up the best to the sous vide process. I love to buy brioche in loaf form and cut it into really thick slices. It looks impressive to pile the toast high on the plate, and it's the perfect canvas to top with fresh fruit or a few slices of bacon. The decadent candied pecans topping takes just a few minutes to put together.

FOR THE FRENCH TOAST

6 large eggs

¼ cup 2% milk

1 teaspoon vanilla extract

1 teaspoon ground cinnamon

2 teaspoons brown sugar

⅛ teaspoon salt

1 teaspoon orange zest (optional)

8 (2-inch-thick) slices brioche bread

4 tablespoons (½ stick) cold unsalted butter, divided

1 cup maple syrup

FOR THE CANDIED PECANS

½ cup brown sugar

¼ teaspoon ground cinnamon

¼ teaspoon salt

1 tablespoon water

½ cup chopped pecans

TO MAKE THE FRENCH TOAST

1. Preheat the sous vide machine to 148°F.

2. In a large mixing bowl, whisk together the eggs, milk, vanilla, cinnamon, sugar, salt, and orange zest (if using) until well combined.

3. Dip the bread in the egg mixture, soaking it thoroughly. Place 4 pieces of of soaked bread in each of two (gallon-size) zip-top bags. Divide any remaining egg mixture between the bags.

4. When the water bath is ready, use the water displacement method (see page 10) to gently lower the French toast into the water while releasing as much air as possible from the bag. Once the air is out, the bag is sealed, and the French toast is fully submerged, use clips or weights to keep the ingredients in the bags fully submerged. Sous vide for 90 minutes. Remove the bags from the water bath and set aside.

5. To finish, in a large skillet over medium-high heat, melt 1 tablespoon of butter at a time and panfry each French toast slice for 1 to 2 minutes per side until a golden-brown crust forms.

6. To serve, stack the French toast high on plates, and top with the candied pecans and maple syrup.

CONTINUED

TO MAKE THE CANDIED PECANS

1. While the French toast is cooking, line a rimmed baking sheet with parchment paper.

2. In a small frying pan over medium heat, combine the brown sugar, cinnamon, salt, and water. Whisk the mixture together for 2 minutes until the sugar dissolves, then add the chopped pecans. Stir regularly for 3 minutes, removing from the heat earlier if the pecans start to burn. Pour the mixture onto the prepared baking sheet to dry and cool.

JALAPEÑO PICKLED EGGS

Serves 6	Prep time: 5 minutes	Cook time: 40 minutes	Finishing time: 15 minutes, plus 1 week to pickle

I like to assemble farmer-style plates, also known as "ploughman's lunch" plates, with these addictive jalapeño pickled eggs. I cut them into quarters and arrange them on a platter with chopped seasonal vegetables, pickles, mustard, cheese, ham, butter, and slices of artisan bread. My husband and I look forward to grazing on this simple but satisfying DIY-style snack on lazy Sunday afternoons. With the jalapeño pickled eggs cooked and ready to eat in the refrigerator, prep for the tasty smorgasbord only takes a minute or two. To make these eggs in large batches, I use a 1-quart mason jar.

12 large eggs

1½ cups white vinegar

1½ cups water

1 tablespoon peppercorns

1 tablespoon salt

1 tablespoon sugar

3 garlic cloves, chopped

1 teaspoon red
pepper flakes

1 sliced jalapeño pepper

2 tablespoons finely
chopped fresh dill

1. Preheat the sous vide machine to 150°F.

2. Carefully place the eggs (in their shells) in the bottom of the machine and sous vide for 40 minutes. When done, transfer the eggs to an ice bath for 5 minutes to stop the cooking process. Leave the eggs in their shells.

3. To finish, in a medium saucepan over high heat, combine the white vinegar, water, peppercorns, salt, sugar, garlic, and red pepper flakes. Bring to a boil, then reduce the heat to medium-low and let the mixture simmer for 5 minutes until the sugar dissolves. Remove from the heat and let cool for 10 minutes.

4. Shell each hardboiled egg and place them, with the sliced jalapeño pepper and dill, in a 1-quart mason jar. Pour the cooled pickling liquid into the mason jar until the eggs are fully submerged. Close the lid and refrigerate for 1 week.

PREP TIP Enjoy any leftover pickling liquid as a brine for proteins.

CHAPTER THREE

find recipe on page 42

VEGETABLES

Just as sous vide meat is tender and juicy because the juices stay in the bag, the same is true for vegetables. All the flavor and vitamins remain with the vegetables, retaining their taste and nutritional value.

Preparing and freezing vegetables to sous vide has become a regular habit of mine. I vacuum seal fresh, seasonal veggies and potatoes with fresh herbs so they are ready to sous vide at the end of the week, when my refrigerator is running out of food.

I've included some of my favorite recipes for root vegetables. There are so many fun ways to sous vide potatoes and beets for intensely flavored side dishes. You'll also find ways to sous vide onions to top salads, and garlic to make some of the best garlic bread you've ever eaten. There are recipes to incorporate in the holiday seasons, and pickling recipes to enjoy with a cheese board.

What you won't find are vegetables that really don't work. Some veggies just become too mushy during the process or the flavors aren't meaningful enough to justify the extra sous vide time.

Vegetables cook at a higher temperature than most other sous vide foods. I recommend placing a cutting board or other barrier between the sous vide bath container and any natural stone countertops to protect them from cracking.

VEGETABLES

BALSAMIC BRUSSELS SPROUTS

Serves 4   Prep time: 10 minutes | Cook time: 1 hour | Finishing time: 10 minutes

Brussels sprouts from a sous vide machine are a cut above Brussels sprouts prepared any other way. Cooked to perfection, these vitamin-packed morsels turn out firm but significantly softened compared to their original texture. A quick fry or blast under the broiler crisps them up, then a drizzle of balsamic glaze adds the final touch.

1 pound Brussels sprouts, outer leaves removed, halved

½ cup (1 stick) butter, cubed

3 tablespoons diced fresh garlic

2 teaspoons salt

½ tablespoon olive oil

1 tablespoon freshly squeezed lemon juice

2 teaspoons balsamic glaze

1. Preheat the sous vide machine to 185°F.
2. Vacuum seal the Brussels sprouts in a flat layer with the cubed butter, garlic, and salt, and drop the bag into the sous vide bath for 60 minutes. When done, carefully remove the bag from the hot water and shock the bag in an ice bath for 2 minutes. Remove the Brussels sprouts from the bag and pat dry—very, very dry!
3. Preheat the broiler to high. Line a rimmed baking sheet with parchment paper.
4. Transfer the Brussels sprouts to the prepared baking sheet and brush with the olive oil. Broil the sprouts for 3 to 5 minutes.
5. Plate and serve with the squeezed lemon juice and a drizzle of balsamic glaze.

PREP TIP The Brussels sprouts may float, so use something to weigh them down so they remain fully underwater while cooking. Commercial sous vide weights won't crack in the hot water.

GARLIC CHIVE MASHED POTATOES

Serves 4 to 6   Prep time: 10 minutes | Cook time: 1 hour, 30 minutes | Finishing time: 5 minutes

Mashed potatoes are one of my favorite side dishes to sous vide. They are great any night of the week and a wonderful way to incorporate this cooking method into holiday meals. Guests "ooh" and "ahh" at how creamy, garlicky, and marvelously smooth these potatoes turn out. Another reason this recipe is a favorite is that it's simple to prepare and easy to clean up. The potatoes are cooked in the bag, mashed in the bag, and ready to serve within moments.

2 pounds russet potatoes, peeled and cut into 2-inch chunks

3 tablespoons diced garlic

2 tablespoons diced shallots

½ cup unsalted butter, at room temperature, plus 2 tablespoons

½ cup cream

2 rosemary sprigs

1 teaspoon salt

½ teaspoon freshly ground black pepper

¼ cup diced fresh chives

1. Preheat the sous vide machine to 195°F.

2. Combine the potatoes, garlic, shallots, ½ cup of butter, cream, rosemary, salt, and pepper in a bag and drop the bag into the sous vide bath for 1 hour, 30 minutes. When done, carefully remove the bag from the hot water. Using a kitchen towel, gently massage any remaining lumps of potatoes. If liquid remains in the bag, cut a corner off the bag and strain the potatoes over a mesh sieve. If the mashed potatoes don't have excess liquid in the bag, pour them into a bowl or onto a serving platter. Discard the rosemary sprigs.

3. To finish, top with the remaining 2 tablespoons of butter and the chives.

PREP TIP Mashed potatoes look beautiful with a sprinkle of green. Instead of chives, try parsley or the diced green parts of a scallion.

MEXICAN-STYLE CORN ON THE COB

Serves 4   Prep time: 5 minutes | Cook time: 30 minutes | Finishing time: 5 minutes

Corn cooked sous vide style is ready to be eaten right out of the bag, but I love finishing it on the grill when we barbecue. Corn on the cob is one of the fastest sous vide recipes, and the flavor of the corn is unsurpassed by any other method of cooking.

4 ears of corn, shucked

4 tablespoons (½ stick) cold unsalted butter

1 teaspoon salt

Freshly ground black pepper

¼ cup cotija cheese

1 lime, cut into wedges

1 tablespoon finely chopped fresh cilantro

1. Preheat the sous vide machine to 182°F.
2. Vacuum seal the corn, butter, and salt in a flat layer and drop the bag into the sous vide bath for 30 minutes. When done, carefully remove the bag from the hot water and remove the corn from the bag.
3. Enjoy as is, or finish by grilling on high heat, rotating a couple times, every 30 to 60 seconds, to get some grill marks on the corn.
4. Plate and serve with pepper, the cotija cheese, a squeeze of lime, and the fresh cilantro.

SUBSTITUTION TIP You can swap in queso fresco for the cotija cheese.

PARMESAN GARLIC HERB FRIES

Serves 4 Prep time: 5 minutes | Cook time: 30 minutes | Finishing time: 10 minutes

During our Bay Area days, my husband and I regularly went to Treasure Island, off the coast of San Francisco, for a food truck get-together. That's where our addiction to Parmesan garlic herb fries began. One food truck served them so loaded with garlic that we thought it was a mistake. But we kept ordering them, and they always came with a heaping mass of garlic, and we have made them at home that way ever since. These garlic herb fries are great with ketchup, but I personally love eating them with malt vinegar. In this recipe, I use duck fat, but you can use unsalted butter instead.

6 cups (½-inch wedges) russet potatoes

¼ cup duck fat

4 garlic cloves

2 teaspoons salt, divided

1 tablespoon olive oil

1 tablespoon diced garlic

1 teaspoon freshly ground black pepper

1 cup grated Parmesan cheese

3 tablespoons finely chopped fresh parsley

Ketchup

1. Preheat the sous vide machine to 185°F.
2. Vacuum seal the potato wedges in a flat layer with the duck fat, garlic cloves, and 1 teaspoon of salt. Drop the bag into the sous vide bath for 30 minutes. When done, remove from the hot water and remove the potatoes from the bag. Pat dry and set aside.
3. To finish, preheat the broiler to high. Line a rimmed baking sheet with parchment paper.
4. Brush the potatoes with the olive oil. Arrange them on the prepared baking sheet and broil for 3 to 5 minutes until crisp and brown.
5. In a bowl, mix together the hot fries, garlic, remaining 1 teaspoon of salt, pepper, Parmesan cheese, and parsley.
6. Plate and serve with ketchup.

ASPARAGUS WITH TOASTED ALMONDS

Serves 4　Prep time: 5 minutes | Cook time: 10 minutes | Finishing time: 5 minutes

Asparagus turns out tender yet crisp when cooked sous vide style. It's ready to enjoy right out of the bag, and it is easy to make in advance to pair with other sous vide proteins. This preparation is a little fancier than plain ole asparagus, making it an ideal dish for brunch or a holiday.

1 bunch asparagus

1 tablespoon chopped garlic

1 tablespoon cold unsalted butter

½ teaspoon salt

½ cup sliced almonds

½ lemon, cut into wedges

2 tablespoons freshly grated Parmesan cheese

2 teaspoons freshly ground black pepper

1. Preheat the sous vide machine to 180°F.

2. Season the asparagus with the garlic, butter, and salt.

3. Vacuum seal the asparagus in a flat layer and drop the bag into the sous vide bath for 6 minutes for thin asparagus (½-inch thick), or 9 minutes for thick asparagus (1-inch thick).

4. While the asparagus is cooking, put the almonds (without oil or butter) into a pan over medium heat. Toast, stirring regularly, for about 3 minutes. Remove from the heat before they brown. Set aside.

5. When the asparagus is done, carefully remove the bag from the hot water and remove the asparagus from the bag.

6. To finish, plate the asparagus and serve with the toasted almonds, a squeeze of lemon, and the Parmesan and pepper.

SESAME GREEN BEANS

Serves 4 Prep time: 5 minutes | Cook time: 45 minutes | Finishing time: 15 minutes

These green beans are firm, tender, and crisp. They are a very versatile sous vide vegetable, and they taste great right out of the bag. Make multiple bags of beans and spruce them up with different sauces to complement any proteins on the menu. These beans are a great side for holiday meals, crab cakes, scallops, and chicken.

1 pound green
  beans, trimmed

2 teaspoons diced
  fresh garlic

2 tablespoons cold
  unsalted butter

2 tablespoons Sesame
  Sauce (page 156)

1 tablespoon
  sesame seeds

1. Preheat the sous vide machine to 180°F.

2. Vacuum seal the green beans with the garlic and butter in a flat layer and drop the bag into the sous vide bath for 45 minutes. When done, carefully remove the bag from the hot water and shock the bag in an ice bath for 2 minutes. Remove the green beans from the bag.

3. To finish, plate the green beans and drizzle with the Sesame Sauce and sprinkle with sesame seeds.

PREP TIP Contrast the bright green of the beans with a neutral-colored protein such as chicken, white fish, or salmon.

SPICY TOMATO GARLIC BRUSCHETTA

Serves 4 to 6 Prep time: 5 minutes | Cook time: 45 minutes | Finishing time: 15 minutes

Bruschetta is the perfect make-ahead appetizer for a party or to take to a friend's house or enjoy on a lazy Sunday afternoon. This version is made with garlic tomatoes that you might just start eating straight out of the sous vide bag with a spoon! It's perfect on crusty bread—try a fresh Italian or French loaf.

12 Roma tomatoes

2 tablespoons diced fresh garlic

1 tablespoon diced fresh thyme

1 teaspoon salt

3 tablespoons olive oil, divided

1 large baguette

1 tablespoon finely chopped fresh basil

1 tablespoon balsamic glaze

1. Preheat the sous vide machine to 140°F.

2. Vacuum seal the tomatoes, garlic, thyme, salt, and 2 tablespoons of olive oil in a flat layer and drop the bag into the sous vide bath for 45 minutes. When done, carefully remove the bag from the hot water and shock the bag in an ice bath for 2 minutes. Open the bag and strain the tomatoes over a mesh sieve. Discard any excess liquid.

3. To finish, roughly chop the tomatoes into bite-size chunks. Set aside.

4. Preheat the oven to 400°F. Line a baking sheet with parchment paper.

5. Slice the baguette diagonally into ½-inch slices. Brush the slices with the remaining 1 tablespoon of olive oil. Bake for about 10 minutes or until the bread is lightly toasted.

6. Top each toast with a spoonful of tomatoes. Sprinkle each with basil and drizzle with balsamic glaze.

CINNAMON SWEET POTATO FRIES

Serves 4   Prep time: 5 minutes | Cook time: 45 minutes | Finishing time: 10 minutes

This method of cooking sweet potatoes leaves them light and fluffy on the inside but crispy on the outside. If you've never dipped fries in honey mustard sauce, you really have to try it. In this recipe, the flavor combination is even more elevated with a dusting of sweet and slightly spicy brown sugar. Don't invite too many friends over to enjoy these with you because you probably won't want to share.

6 cups sweet potatoes, cut into ½-inch sticks

4 tablespoons (½ stick) cold unsalted butter

2 teaspoons salt, divided

¼ teaspoon ground cinnamon

¼ teaspoon ground cumin

1 tablespoon brown sugar

½ teaspoon freshly ground black pepper

1 tablespoon olive oil

3 tablespoons honey mustard

1. Preheat the sous vide machine to 185°F.

2. Vacuum seal the sweet potatoes, butter, and 1 teaspoon of salt in a flat layer and drop the bag into the sous vide bath for 45 minutes. When done, carefully remove the bag from the hot water. Remove the sweet potatoes from the bag and pat dry. Set aside.

3. To finish, preheat the oven broiler to high. Line a baking sheet with parchment paper.

4. In a small mixing bowl, mix together the cinnamon, cumin, brown sugar, remaining 1 teaspoon of salt, and pepper. Set aside.

5. Brush the sweet potatoes with the olive oil. Arrange the sweet potatoes on the prepared baking sheet and sprinkle with the spice mix.

6. Broil for 3 to 5 minutes until the fries are crisp and brown.

7. Plate and serve with the honey mustard for dipping.

PREP TIP To finish these fries on the grill, spray them with olive oil cooking spray and place them perpendicular to the grill lines so they don't fall through. Turn them after about 1 minute, after grill marks form.

BEET SALAD WITH ARUGULA

Serves 4 | Prep time: 5 minutes | Cook time: 3 hours, 15 minutes | Finishing time: 5 minutes

This is one of my favorite make-ahead lunches. Sous vide beets are easy to prepare in advance and enjoy for days. This method of cooking them retains more nutrients and creates a deep flavor. They're also a perfect texture—soft and tender but easily pierced with a fork. Enjoy them warm or chilled in a salad such as this one.

FOR THE DRESSING

⅓ cup champagne vinegar

⅓ cup olive oil

1 teaspoon honey

1 teaspoon freshly grated orange zest

¼ teaspoon garlic salt

¼ teaspoon freshly ground black pepper

FOR THE BEETS AND SALAD

8 (4-inch-diameter) red beets, quartered

3 thyme sprigs

3 tablespoons cold unsalted butter

4 cups arugula

2 tablespoons diced shallots

¼ cup hazelnuts

½ cup crumbled blue cheese

Freshly ground black pepper

TO MAKE THE DRESSING

In a medium mixing bowl, combine the vinegar, olive oil, honey, orange zest, garlic salt, and pepper. Whisk together until thoroughly combined. Set aside.

TO COOK THE BEETS AND PREPARE THE SALAD

1. Preheat the sous vide machine to 185°F.

2. Vacuum seal the beets with the thyme and butter in a flat layer and drop the bag into the sous vide bath for 3 hours, 15 minutes. When done, remove the beets from the hot water and shock the bag in an ice bath for 2 minutes. Strain the beets in a metal sieve and discard the excess juice.

3. To finish, dress the beets and plate them on top of the arugula on a large serving platter or on individual plates. Top with the shallots, hazelnuts, blue cheese, and pepper.

PREP TIP It's important not to mix the blue cheese with the beets, but to sprinkle the blue cheese on top of the salad. Mixing the two together will discolor the blue cheese.

WARM SPINACH SALAD WITH FETA CHEESE AND ONIONS

Serves 4 to 6 | Prep time: 5 minutes | Cook time: 2 hours | Finishing time: 10 minutes

Onions add the perfect finishing touch to many dishes. I particularly love them in this warm spinach salad. The spinach isn't actually cooked. Instead, the warm onions wilt the spinach as it's served. Since the onions are so beautiful, let them sit on top, waiting for you to dig in with a fork.

4 yellow onions, halved, then cut into ½-inch half circles

2 rosemary sprigs

3 tablespoons cold unsalted butter

½ teaspoon salt

FOR THE DRESSING

⅓ cup red wine vinegar

⅓ cup olive oil

1 teaspoon honey

1 teaspoon stone ground mustard

1 teaspoon freshly grated lemon zest

¼ teaspoon garlic salt

¼ teaspoon freshly ground black pepper

FOR THE SALAD

1 pound fresh spinach

1 cup cherry tomatoes, halved

½ cup crumbled goat cheese, or feta

¼ cup chopped hazelnuts

Freshly ground black pepper

1. Preheat the sous vide machine to 185°F.

2. Vacuum seal the onions, rosemary, butter, and salt in a flat layer and drop the bag into the sous vide bath for 2 hours. When done, carefully remove the bag from the hot water, and pour the onions and juice from the bag into a medium saucepan over medium heat. Discard the rosemary.

3. To finish, heat the onions until the juice evaporates, about 5 minutes.

TO MAKE THE DRESSING

In a medium mixing bowl, whisk together the vinegar, olive oil, honey, mustard, lemon zest, garlic salt, and pepper until well combined.

TO MAKE THE SALAD

In a large bowl, toss the spinach with the dressing and plate it on a large serving platter or on individual plates. Top with the onions, followed by the tomatoes, feta, hazelnuts, and pepper to taste.

CHEESY CIABATTA BREAD WITH GARLIC SPREAD

Serves 4   Prep time: 5 minutes | Cook time: 5 hours | Finishing time: 10 minutes

Here's an addictive appetizer for a party or a side for your favorite Italian fare. Sous vide garlic is great with a variety of flavors. For a shortcut, use whole garlic cloves with skins removed to make this sous vide garlic. You'll also need a pint-size mason jar in which to cook the garlic and olive oil. Try variations of this recipe by adding parsley, dill, oregano, or jalapeño peppers.

½ cup garlic
   cloves, peeled

½ teaspoon salt

1 rosemary sprig

1 thyme sprig

¼ cup olive oil

½ cup butter, at
   room temperature

¼ cup freshly grated
   Parmesan cheese

1 large loaf
   ciabatta bread,
   halved lengthwise

1 cup shredded
   mozzarella cheese

2 tablespoons chopped
   fresh parsley

1. Preheat the sous vide machine to 190°F.

2. Put the garlic in a pint-size mason jar with the salt, rosemary, and thyme. Fill the jar with olive oil and drop it into the sous vide bath for 5 hours. When done, use tongs to carefully remove the jar from the hot water.

3. To finish, preheat the oven broiler to high. Line a baking sheet with parchment paper.

4. Transfer the garlic and olive oil to a medium mixing bowl. Discard the used rosemary and thyme sprigs. Add the butter and Parmesan cheese to the bowl and mix together to form a paste. Set aside.

5. Place the bread on the prepared baking sheet and use a spatula to spread the paste on the bread. Top with the mozzarella cheese.

6. Broil for 2 to 4 minutes or until the cheese is bubbly.

7. Plate and serve sprinkled with the parsley.

PREP TIP Make the garlic spread up to 5 days in advance.

GARLICKY BUTTERED LITTLE POTATOES WITH ROSEMARY

Serves 4 | Prep time: 5 minutes | Cook time: 60 minutes | Finishing time: 5 minutes

I just can't resist picking up a bag of little potatoes whenever I pass them in the grocery store. They are so cute, and they make a very attractive potato appetizer when presented with fresh herbs in a white serving dish. The fragrant rosemary in this recipe makes these sous vide little potatoes perfect for a holiday gathering, but they are easy enough to throw together for any night of the week. The result of the sous vide process leaves the potatoes as smooth as butter. If you're also a huge fan of little potatoes, you'll love how these turn out.

1 pound small (2- to 3-inch) skin-on potatoes, washed

2 tablespoons cold unsalted butter

1 tablespoon olive oil

1 tablespoon minced garlic

2 rosemary sprigs, plus 1 teaspoon diced fresh rosemary

1 teaspoon salt

1 teaspoon freshly ground black pepper

¼ lemon

1. Preheat the sous vide bath to 190°F.

2. Vacuum seal the potatoes, butter, olive oil, garlic, rosemary sprigs, salt, and pepper in a flat layer in a sous vide bag and drop the bag into the sous vide bath for 60 minutes. When done, carefully remove the bag from the hot water.

3. To finish, transfer the potatoes to a serving dish. Discard the rosemary sprigs. Squeeze the lemon over the potatoes, sprinkle with the diced rosemary, and serve.

SUBSTITUTION TIP This recipe can be made using regular-size Yukon Gold potatoes. To substitute, dice the Yukon Golds into 2-inch chunks before vacuum sealing them.

CUCUMBER PICKLES

Serves 10 | Prep time: 10 minutes | Cook time: 2 hours, 30 minutes | Finishing time: 1 hour

This recipe makes four 1-pint mason jars of pickles. Scale up to make as gifts for the holidays or to share with friends and coworkers. Enjoy these pickles straight from the jar, on sous vide burgers, sandwiches, and cheese plates. Once you master pickling, it's easy to swap out different flavors. Try using other herbs, such as rosemary, or add some heat with red pepper flakes or jalapeño peppers.

2 cups water

2 cups white wine vinegar

⅓ cup sugar

2 tablespoons pickling salt

8 dill sprigs

4 bay leaves

5 cups Persian cucumbers, cut into ½-inch disks

1 red onion, halved and cut into ½-inch half circles

1 tablespoon diced garlic

1 tablespoon black or green peppercorns

1 teaspoon red pepper flakes

1. Preheat the sous vide machine to 140°F.

2. In a medium mixing bowl, mix together the water, vinegar, sugar, and salt until the solids dissolve. Set aside.

3. Place 2 dill sprigs and 1 bay leaf in each jar. Then equally distribute the cucumbers, onion, garlic, peppercorns, and red pepper flakes among the jars, leaving at least 2 inches of space at the top of each jar.

4. Fill the jars with the brine, leaving a 1-inch space at the top of each jar.

5. Screw on the lids just enough so they are sealed. Over-tightening the lids may result in cracked glass. Place the pickle jars in the sous vide bath for 2 hours, 30 minutes. When done, carefully remove the jars from the hot water. Do not cool them in an ice bath, which may crack the glass. Let cool for 1 hour before refrigerating.

SUBSTITUTION TIP A fine pure sea salt may be used in place of pickling salt.

PICKLED CURRY ZUCCHINI CHIPS

Serves 10   Prep time: 10 minutes | Cook time: 2 hours, 30 minutes | Finishing time: 1 hour

This recipe makes four 1-pint mason jars of pickles. The inspiration for this comes from one of my favorite charcuterie bars in Portland. Before we started making them at home, we used to pick up pickled zucchini when ordering craft sausage. Zucchini is great to pickle because it is like a sponge, soaking up different flavors. It produces a floppier pickle—one that's great for burgers and sandwiches. In this version, zucchini is paired with curry seasoning and red peppers. The ingredients look beautiful together in the pickling jar. This recipe is always a hit on cheese platters and is a fun way to introduce friends and family to both sous vide cooking and pickled zucchini.

2 cups water

2 cups white
  wine vinegar

⅓ cup sugar

2 tablespoons
  pickling salt

4 bay leaves

5 cups (trimmed and
  cut into ¼-inch
  disks) zucchini

1 cup sliced red
  bell pepper

2 tablespoons
  diced shallots

1 tablespoon black or
  green peppercorns

1½ teaspoons
  ground cardamom

2 teaspoons
  curry powder

1 teaspoon turmeric

½ teaspoon red
  pepper flakes

1. Preheat the sous vide machine to 140°F.

2. In a medium mixing bowl, mix together the water, vinegar, sugar, and salt until the solids dissolve. Set aside.

3. Put 1 bay leaf in each jar. Then equally distribute the zucchini, bell pepper, shallots, peppercorns, cardamom, curry powder, turmeric, and red pepper flakes among the jars, leaving at least 2 inches of space at the top of each jar.

4. Fill the jars with the brine, leaving a 1-inch space at the top of each jar.

5. Screw on the lids just enough so they are sealed. Overtightening the lids may result in cracked glass. Place the pickle jars in the sous vide bath for 2 hours, 30 minutes. When done, carefully remove the pickle jars from the hot water. Do not cool them in an ice bath, which may crack the glass. Let cool for 1 hour before refrigerating.

SUBSTITUTION TIP Carrots are a great substitute for zucchini in this recipe.

CHAPTER FOUR

find recipe on page 59

SEAFOOD

One of the frustrating aspects of cooking seafood at home is that it can overcook easily—it can dry out on the grill or in the oven. And on the stove, you can't determine the exact temperature of the pan, so it's easy to burn.

But you can put your mind at ease when using sous vide to cook seafood. Delicate and pricey fish, lobster, scallops, shrimp, and crab slowly cooking at the specific temperature controlled by the sous vide machine means there is no way to ruin dinner. You simply have to try sous vide lobster! It melts in your mouth, just as you'd expect at a fine restaurant.

For dinner parties and other social events, prepping seafood first in the sous vide bath means it can be made ahead, then finished on the grill, broiled in the oven, or flash-seared on the stove when it's time to eat. Sous vide is also a great way to make bacon-wrapped scallops for an appetizer and grilled shrimp rice bowls as main dishes.

In this chapter, you'll learn how to prepare seafood that is usually available at most fish counters. You'll be impressed by the tender and intensely flavored seafood this cooking method can produce.

SEAFOOD

LOBSTER WITH BEURRE BLANC SAUCE

Serves 4   Prep time: 5 minutes | Cook time: 25 minutes | Finishing time: 5 minutes

Here's a recipe for date-night-in, although any night can feel special with easy but fancy lobster prepared sous vide style. The lobster tails are poached in butter and paired with a beurre blanc sauce that is creamy, simple, and light. To save on prep time, ask your fishmonger to de-shell the lobsters at the time of purchase.

FOR THE LOBSTERS

4 (1½-pound) lobster tails, de-shelled

½ teaspoon salt

½ teaspoon freshly ground black pepper

2 teaspoons diced garlic

3 tarragon sprigs

4 tablespoons (½ stick) unsalted butter

FOR THE BEURRE BLANC SAUCE

¼ cup dry white wine (try Chardonnay)

¼ cup white wine vinegar

1 cup diced onion

2 tablespoons diced shallot

1 tablespoon diced garlic

⅓ cup heavy (whipping) cream

1 cup (2 sticks) unsalted butter

½ lemon

Salt

Freshly ground black pepper

TO SOUS VIDE THE LOBSTERS

1. Preheat the sous vide machine to 134°F.
2. Season the lobster tails with the salt, pepper, and garlic. Vacuum seal the tails, tarragon, and butter, and drop the bag into the sous vide bath for 25 minutes. When done, carefully remove the bag from the water and shock the bag in an ice bath for 2 minutes. Remove the lobster tails from the bag and pat dry.

TO MAKE THE BEURRE BLANC SAUCE

1. In a medium saucepan over medium heat, combine the white wine, vinegar, onion, shallot, and garlic and cook, whisking regularly, for 5 minutes until the liquid reduces by half. Add the heavy cream, turn the heat to medium-high, and boil the sauce for 1 minute. Continue whisking while adding the butter, 1 tablespoon at a time. After about a minute, the sauce should be creamy and smooth. Turn off the heat when the sauce can easily coat the back of a spoon. Squeeze the lemon half over the sauce and season with salt and pepper as desired.
2. Using a wire mesh sieve, strain the sauce into a spouted dish or gravy bowl. Discard the leftover bits of garlic, shallots, and onion.

FOR FINISHING

8 cups salad

Greens (optional)

1 lemon, quartered

1 tablespoon finely
  chopped fresh parsley

TO FINISH

1. Slice the lobster tails into 1-inch disks and set
   them on plates lined with salad greens (if using)
   or directly on a serving platter.

2. Squeeze the lemon wedges over the lobster and
   sprinkle with the parsley.

3. Drizzle the beurre blanc sauce on top of the lobster, or serve the sauce on the side.

BLACKENED SCALLOPS

Serves 4   Prep time: 5 minutes | Cook time: 30 minutes | Finishing time: 5 minutes

The first trip my husband and I took as a couple was to New Orleans. At the time, he was a chef at a Cajun restaurant in Baltimore, and we were both thrilled to embark on our first foodie adventure together. What a wonderful city to explore by mouth and foot. Ever since, we've kept an industrial-size container of blackening seasoning in our pantry. This recipe is one of our favorite ways to enjoy the flavors and reminisce about that first trip together.

12 large (2-inch diameter) scallops

1 teaspoon diced garlic

2 teaspoons blackening seasoning

½ tablespoon olive oil

1 tablespoon diced fresh parsley

1. Preheat the sous vide machine to 123°F.

2. Coat the scallops with the garlic and blackening seasoning. Vacuum seal the scallops in a flat layer and drop the bag into the sous vide bath for 30 minutes. When done, carefully remove the bag from the hot water and shock the bag in an ice bath for 2 minutes. Remove the scallops from the bag and pat dry.

3. To finish, in a medium cast iron skillet over medium-high heat, heat the olive oil until it is shimmering. Add the scallops and sear each side for 1 to 2 minutes until lightly browned. Remove from the heat and sprinkle with the parsley.

PREP TIP   Serve blackened scallops over a simple salad with a champagne vinaigrette, quinoa, or rice.

HERBY SHRIMP LINGUINE IN WHITE WINE SAUCE

Serves 4   Prep time: 5 minutes | Cook time: 15 minutes | Finishing time: 10 minutes

Unlike some other sous vide recipes, sous vide shrimp has a small window of cook time. That means it's an easy weeknight dinner and becomes a complete meal when paired with pasta in a tasty white wine sauce. I like to serve this dish family-style, in a large cast iron skillet, so everyone can dig in and enjoy seconds and, sometimes, thirds!

FOR THE SHRIMP

1 pound (3-inch) shrimp, peeled and deveined

½ teaspoon salt

1 tablespoon diced garlic

1 teaspoon dried fennel

1 teaspoon dried sage

½ teaspoon red pepper flakes

FOR THE LINGUINE

1 pound linguine

1 teaspoon olive oil

TO SOUS VIDE THE SHRIMP

1. Preheat the sous vide machine to 130°F.
2. In a bowl, coat the shrimp with the salt, garlic, fennel, sage, and red pepper flakes. Vacuum seal the shrimp in a flat layer and drop the bag into the sous vide bath for 15 minutes. When the shrimp are done, remove them from the hot water and shock the bag in an ice bath for 2 minutes. Remove the shrimp from the bag and pat dry.

TO MAKE THE LINGUINE

Bring a large pot of water to a boil. Add the linguini and boil until al dente. Make sure not to overcook the pasta because it will cook a little more when added to the sauce. Once done, drain the pasta and toss with the olive oil so the pasta doesn't stick together, and set aside.

CONTINUED

FOR FINISHING

1 tablespoon olive oil

4 tablespoons
(½ stick) cold unsalted
butter, divided

4 garlic cloves, diced

2 shallots, diced

1½ cups dry white wine
(try Chardonnay)

4 tablespoons freshly
squeezed lemon juice

3 tablespoons
capers, drained

½ cup diced fresh parsley

Salt

Freshly ground
black pepper

½ cup grated
Parmesan cheese

1 tablespoon chopped
fresh basil

TO FINISH

1. In a large pan with deep sides over medium-high heat, heat the olive oil until it is shimmering. Add the shrimp to the pan and brown on each side for 1 minute. Remove the shrimp from the pan.

2. Reduce the heat to medium. Add 2 tablespoons of butter, the garlic, and shallots. Stir regularly for 1 minute, making sure the garlic does not burn. Add the white wine and whisk the sauce for 1 to 2 minutes until the liquid has reduced by half. Add the lemon juice and whisk for 1 minute.

3. Reduce the heat to medium-low. Add the remaining 2 tablespoons of butter, the capers, parsley, and al dente pasta to the white wine sauce. Season with salt and pepper. Add the shrimp to the sauce and let it simmer for 2 minutes. Sprinkle with the Parmesan, top with the basil, and serve.

MAKE IT EASY TIP Refrigerate leftover shrimp in the refrigerator for 3 to 4 days in an airtight container.

LEMON-HERB TUNA

Serves 4   Prep time: 5 minutes | Cook time: 40 minutes | Finishing time: 10 minutes

This recipe came about after I went to the grocery store without a list. The tuna looked great, and I asked the fishmonger for a recommendation on how to enjoy it. He inspired me to prep the tuna with some herbs and lemon, and we've been eating tuna sous vide style with this seasoning ever since. It's wonderful for home chefs looking to cook foolproof rare tuna, as the sous vide process ensures the tuna is perfectly cooked edge to edge.

½ teaspoon garlic salt

¼ teaspoon freshly ground black pepper

¼ teaspoon dried oregano, divided

¼ teaspoon dried thyme, divided

¼ teaspoon dried basil, divided

4 tuna fillets

1 tablespoon olive oil

1 lemon, seeded and thinly sliced

1 tablespoon diced fresh basil

1. Preheat the sous vide machine to 110°F.

2. In a bowl, mix together the garlic salt, pepper, oregano, thyme, and basil. Season the tuna with the spice mix and top with half the lemon slices.

3. Vacuum seal the tuna fillets in a flat layer and drop the bag into the sous vide bath for 40 minutes. When done, carefully remove the bag from the water bath and shock the bag in an ice bath for 2 minutes. Remove the tuna from the bag and pat dry.

4. To finish, pour the olive oil into a medium cast iron skillet over high heat. When the oil is shimmering, add the tuna and sear each side for 15 to 45 seconds. Remove from the heat and sprinkle with the basil. Garnish with the remaining lemon slices.

EASY-PEASY JUMBO SHRIMP COCKTAIL

Serves 4   Prep time: 5 minutes | Cook time: 60 minutes | Finishing time: 5 minutes

Entertaining with sous vide doesn't get much easier than this. This appetizer is ready to go at a moment's notice because it uses frozen jumbo shrimp. It is best made on the day of the event, then kept refrigerated until serving. Since I'm from Baltimore, I like to season shrimp cocktail with Old Bay. You can add any seasoning you like during the sous vide process, even good ole salt and pepper. Baking soda, which I like to use when serving shrimp cocktail, keeps the shrimp firm, which is great since it isn't finished in a cast iron skillet or on the grill.

1 pound extra-large
   jumbo shrimp

⅛ teaspoon salt

⅛ teaspoon freshly
   ground black pepper

½ teaspoon baking soda

2 teaspoons Old Bay
   seasoning, or your
   choice (optional)

1 lemon, cut into wedges

FOR THE COCKTAIL SAUCE

1 cup ketchup

2 tablespoons freshly
   squeezed lemon juice

3 teaspoons
   horseradish, drained

¼ teaspoon
   Worcestershire sauce

¼ teaspoon
   Tabasco sauce

1. Preheat the sous vide machine to 135°F.

2. In a bowl, coat the frozen jumbo shrimp with the salt, pepper, baking soda, and seasoning (if using). Vacuum seal the shrimp in a flat layer and drop the bag into the sous vide bath for 60 minutes. When the shrimp are done, carefully remove the bag from the hot water and shock the bag in an ice bath for 2 minutes. Remove the shrimp from the bag and pat dry. Set aside.

3. Serve the shrimp with the cocktail sauce and lemon wedges.

TO MAKE THE COCKTAIL SAUCE

In a medium mixing bowl, mix together the ketchup, lemon juice, horseradish, Worcestershire sauce, and Tabasco sauce until thoroughly combined.

PREP TIP To make this a meal, toss the shrimp with pesto and serve over risotto topped with freshly grated Parmesan cheese.

HONEY-GARLIC SALMON

Serves 4   Prep time: 5 minutes | Cook time: 45 minutes | Finishing time: 5 minutes

Living in the Pacific Northwest, I'm always looking for new ways to take advantage of the fresh and readily available salmon. This dish does it for me. The flavor of the salmon turns out a little smoky, thanks to the smoked salt, and a little sweet, thanks to the Honey-Garlic Sauce. Cooked sous vide style, it's easy to achieve the perfect translucent pink color everyone wants when cooking salmon. And the texture is flaky and smooth. The sauce itself is so addictive, I often make a double batch to enjoy it later in the week on other proteins.

4 salmon fillets

⅛ teaspoon smoked salt

⅛ teaspoon freshly ground black pepper

1 tablespoon diced garlic

2 teaspoons olive oil

¼ cup Honey-Garlic Sauce (page 144)

1. Preheat the sous vide machine to 125°F.

2. Season the salmon with the salt, pepper, and garlic. Vacuum seal the salmon in a flat layer and drop the bag into the sous vide bath for 45 minutes. When done, carefully remove the bag from the hot water and shock the bag in an ice bath for 2 minutes. Remove the salmon from the bag and pat dry. Set aside.

3. To finish, in a medium cast iron skillet over medium-high heat, heat the olive oil until it is shimmering. Add the salmon fillets and sear the skin side only, until crisp, 30 to 60 seconds.

4. Plate each fillet and drizzle with the Honey-Garlic Sauce.

SUBSTITUTION TIP To change up the flavor, make the salmon and serve it with Hollandaise Sauce (page 160).

MEXICAN GRILLED SHRIMP RICE BOWLS

Serves 4   Prep time: 20 minutes | Cook time: 15 minutes | Finishing time: 10 minutes

If you're looking to feed a crowd, you can turn these fun grilled Mexican rice bowls into a DIY Mexican bowl bar. They are spicy, colorful, and packed with flavor. I like to top mine with three to five main ingredients, then I go a bit crazy and garnish them with a little bit of everything—cilantro, lime juice, hot sauce, and cheese. I like to vacuum seal already skewered shrimp on kebab sticks. Prepping the shrimp on the kebab sticks helps keep the shrimp from overlapping in the vacuum-sealed bag and makes it easy to get them from the sous vide bath to the grill.

FOR THE SHRIMP

1 pound (3-inch) shrimp, peeled and deveined

½ teaspoon salt

½ teaspoon freshly ground black pepper

2 teaspoons diced garlic

2 teaspoons diced shallot

1 tablespoon finally chopped fresh cilantro

FOR THE SPICE MIXTURE

1 tablespoon olive oil

½ teaspoon chili powder

¼ teaspoon dried oregano

¼ teaspoon paprika

¼ teaspoon chipotle powder

⅛ teaspoon salt

⅛ teaspoon freshly ground black pepper

TO SOUS VIDE THE SHRIMP

1. Preheat the sous vide machine to 130°F.
2. Skewer 4 or 5 shrimp on each stick, to evenly divide them into 4 servings. Season the shrimp with the salt, pepper, garlic, shallot, and cilantro. Vacuum seal the shrimp in a flat layer and drop the bag into the sous vide bath for 15 minutes. When the shrimp are done, carefully remove the bag from the hot water and shock the bag in an ice bath for 2 minutes. Remove the shrimp from the bag and pat dry.

TO PREPARE THE SPICE MIXTURE

In a small bowl, mix together the olive oil, chili powder, oregano, paprika, chipotle powder, salt, and pepper. Brush the mixture on the shrimp kebabs.

TO FINISH THE BOWLS (PREPARE 3 TO 5)

2 cups cooked rice
  (or cauliflower rice)

2 avocados, pitted
  and diced

1 cup diced tomatoes

1 cup cooked corn

1 cup roasted zucchini

1 cup black
  beans, drained

TOPPINGS

1 cup sour cream

1 cup salsa

1 cup finely chopped
  fresh cilantro

1 cup lime wedges
  (about 1 lime)

1 cup cotija cheese

Hot sauce

Crumbled tortilla chips

TO FINISH

1. Preheat the grill to high and grill the kebabs for 30 to 90 seconds on each side until lightly grilled. It's important not to overcook the outside of the shrimp, as the inside is already cooked to temperature.

2. Assemble the bowls by starting with a layer of rice in each bowl and then layering avocado, tomato, corn, zucchini, and black beans on top. Top with the grilled shrimp skewers and other desired toppings.

MAKE IT EASY For easy grilling, use 2 kebab sticks for each set of skewered shrimp. This will help you flip them on the grill.

HALIBUT WITH SWEET SESAME-GINGER DRESSING

Serves 4 | Prep time: 5 minutes | Cook time: 45 minutes | Finishing time: 5 minutes

Halibut is a lean fish that stands up well to the sous vide process. Once cooked in the bath, it's transformed into a tender and delicate fish, but it remains some-what firm and dense. When I cook white fish such as halibut, I like to serve it with vibrant vegetables to add bold color to the plate. Drizzling Sweet Sesame-Ginger Dressing on the fish and around the plate gives the dish a restaurant feel.

4 halibut fillets

1 teaspoon salt

4 garlic cloves

1 lemongrass
  stalk, halved

¼ cup Sweet
  Sesame-Ginger
  Dressing (page 146)

1. Preheat the sous vide machine to 130°F.

2. Season the halibut with the salt. Use two vacuum seal bags and put 2 fillets, 2 garlic cloves, and 1 lemongrass half in a flat layer in each bag. Drop the bags into the sous vide bath for 45 minutes. When done, carefully remove the bags from the hot water and shock the bags in an ice bath for 2 minutes. Remove the halibut from the bags and pat dry. Set aside.

3. To finish, preheat the oven broiler to high. Line a rimmed baking sheet with parchment paper.

4. Place the halibut on the prepared baking sheet and broil for 1 to 2 minutes until lightly browned.

5. Plate the fish over the vegetables and drizzle with the dressing.

SUBSTITUTION TIP Sous vide halibut is also great paired with balsamic, Dijon vinaigrette, or a lemon cream sauce.

SPICY JERK PRAWNS

Serves 4 | Prep time: 5 minutes | Cook time: 30 minutes | Finishing time: 5 minutes

I collect dishware, kitchen towels, and spices everywhere I go. After cruising the Caribbean, I picked up an amazing jerk seasoning that I've been recreating at home ever since. It really changes up the flavor profile of a dish because it uses not-so-common spices such as cinnamon and nutmeg. One of my favorite ways to use this seasoning is on sweet and meaty prawns, which are easy to find in bulk, often in the freezer section. To balance the flavors of this dish, I recommend serving these spicy prawns with a glass of sweet German Riesling.

2 dozen jumbo prawns, peeled and deveined

2 tablespoons Jerk Seasoning (page 147)

2 teaspoons olive oil

½ lemon, cut into wedges

1 tablespoon finely chopped fresh parsley

1. Preheat the sous vide machine to 130°F.

2. In a small mixing bowl, toss the prawns with the jerk seasoning. Vacuum seal the prawns in a flat layer and drop the bag into the sous vide bath for 30 minutes. When done, carefully remove the bag from the hot water and shock the bag in an ice bath for 2 minutes. Remove the prawns from the bag and pat dry. Set aside.

3. To finish, in a medium cast iron skillet on medium-high heat, heat the olive oil until it is shimmering. Add the prawns and flash sear, 15 to 30 seconds on each side.

4. Plate the prawns with a squeeze of lemon and the fresh parsley.

PREP TIP If cooking prawns from frozen, add ½ teaspoon of baking soda to the vacuum seal bag before cooking in the sous vide bath; doing this will help the prawns plump up.

MEDITERRANEAN COD WITH LEMON-TAHINI SAUCE

Serves 4 Prep time: 5 minutes | Cook time: 30 minutes | Finishing time: 10 minutes

Cod can be a very delicate fish, which means it doesn't always cook easily when prepared with some methods. Cooked sous vide style, cod turns out meaty, flaky, and firm but never overcooked. The sauce on this cod is a cool and refreshing twist on the age-old pairing of lemon and fish. I like to serve cod with potatoes and vegetables because the more ways to enjoy this sauce, the better.

4 cod fillets

1 tablespoon finely chopped fresh dill

1 tablespoon diced garlic

1 teaspoon salt

2 tablespoons cold unsalted butter, cubed, plus 1 tablespoon

¼ cup Lemon-Tahini Sauce (page 148)

1. Preheat the sous vide machine to 130°F.

2. Because the fish is delicate, carefully season the cod with the dill, garlic, and salt. Vacuum seal the cod with 2 tablespoons of butter cubes in a flat layer and drop the bag into the sous vide bath for 30 minutes. When done, carefully remove the bag from the hot water and shock the bag in an ice bath for 2 minutes. Using a spatula, gently remove the cod from the bag and pat dry. Set aside.

3. To finish, in a sauté pan or skillet over medium-high heat, melt the remaining 1 tablespoon of butter. Place the cod in the pan and sear for 30 to 60 seconds until lightly browned.

4. Plate the fish and serve with the Lemon-Tahini Sauce.

STORAGE TIP Because cod is a lean fish, it keeps a little longer in the refrigerator than oily fish. Refrigerate and enjoy it for 3 to 4 days.

"GRILLED" LOBSTER WITH GARLIC-DILL BUTTER

Serves 4 Prep time: 5 minutes | Cook time: 25 minutes | Finishing time: 10 minutes

Because this lobster recipe is finished on the grill, I like to sous vide it at a slightly lower temperature than when I simply poach lobster and plate it right out of the bag. Using this method, the additional time on the grill doesn't overcook the lobster. To fancy this dish up, I make a compound butter out of garlic and dill. There's nothing better than ridiculously buttery lobster, and the addition of the herbs takes this meal to the next level.

4 (1½-pound) lobster tails, de-shelled

½ teaspoon salt

2 teaspoons diced garlic

4 tablespoons unsalted butter, cubed

Olive oil cooking spray

4 tablespoons Garlic-Dill Butter (page 149)

1. Preheat the sous vide machine to 130°F.

2. Season the lobster tails with the salt and garlic. Vacuum seal the lobster topped with the butter and drop the bag into the sous vide bath for 25 minutes. When done, carefully remove the bag from the hot water and shock the bag in an ice bath for 2 minutes. Remove the lobster tails from the bag and pat dry. Set aside.

3. To finish, preheat the grill to 500°F.

4. Lightly spray the lobster with olive oil. Arrange the lobster on the grill, over the heat, cut-side (flesh-side) down. Grill for 1 to 2 minutes, then move the lobster 45 degrees to get crisscross grill marks, and grill for another 1 to 2 minutes.

5. Plate each lobster tail with a pat of Garlic-Dill Butter on top.

LEMONY SEA BASS

Serves 4   Prep time: 5 minutes | Cook time: 30 minutes | Finishing time: 5 minutes

Mild sea bass takes on a bright, refreshing lemony note with this recipe. Cooked sous vide style, sea bass is flaky, meaty, and moist. Since it's already more of a fatty and buttery fish compared with some others, it's not necessary to add butter to the sous vide bag.

4 sea bass fillets

2 teaspoons diced shallot

½ teaspoon salt

1 teaspoon
chopped garlic

2 tablespoons cold
unsalted butter, divided

1 lemon

1. Preheat the sous vide machine to 130°F.

2. Season the sea bass with the shallots, salt, and garlic. Cut half of the lemon into 4 disks. Vacuum seal the sea bass with 1 lemon disk and ¼ tablespoon of butter on each piece of fish in a flat layer and drop the bag into the sous vide bath for 30 minutes. When done, carefully remove the bag from the hot water and shock the bag in an ice bath for 2 minutes. Using a spatula, remove the sea bass from the bag and pat dry. Set aside.

3. To finish, in a sauté pan or skillet over medium-high heat, melt the remaining 1 tablespoon of butter. Place the fillets in the sauté pan or skillet and sear for 30 to 60 seconds, skin-side down, until browned.

4. Plate and serve with a squeeze of lemon from the remaining lemon half.

SERVING TIP Sea bass tastes great with salty and strong flavored ingredients. Try it alongside artichokes, capers, kale, and chard.

BUSY-NIGHT CRAB CAKES (FROM FROZEN)

Serves 4   Prep time: 5 minutes | Cook time: 60 minutes | Finishing time: 5 minutes

I came up with this recipe after I vacuum sealed extra (raw) crab cakes and froze them. It's great if you want to buy in bulk or mail-order frozen crab cakes. Cooking this way means that you're essentially using the sous vide machine to defrost and cook the crab cakes, and it couldn't be easier. To finish them off, sear so they are nice and crispy on the outside.

8 frozen crab cakes

3 tablespoons cold unsalted butter

4 lemons, cut in wedges

1. Preheat the sous vide machine to 150°F.

2. Place the frozen vacuum-sealed crab cakes in a flat layer in a sous vide bag and drop the bag into the sous vide bath for 60 minutes. When done, carefully remove the bag from the hot water and, using a spatula, carefully remove the crab cakes from the bag and set aside on a paper towel.

3. To finish, in a skillet over medium-high heat, melt the butter. Add the crab cakes and sear each side for 2 to 3 minutes until browned. Plate and serve with the lemon wedge.

BUTTERY SOFT-SHELL CRABS

Serves 4   Prep time: 5 minutes | Cook time: 3 hours | Finishing time: 5 minutes

These soft-shell crabs are so tender. They are light, delicate, and buttery, thanks to poaching them sous vide style. This recipe uses Old Bay seasoning, which has been a favorite of mine ever since I lived in Maryland. When you buy the crabs, ask the fishmonger to clean them so they are ready to season and cook. Serve them in sandwiches or on salads.

8 soft-shell crabs

1 tablespoon Old Bay seasoning

4 tablespoons (½ stick) cold unsalted butter, divided

1 tablespoon olive oil

Salt

Freshly ground black pepper

1 lemon, cut into wedges

1. Preheat the sous vide machine to 145°F.

2. In a bowl, season the crabs with the Old Bay seasoning. Vacuum seal the crabs, two to a bag, in a flat layer with 1 tablespoon of butter in each bag and drop the bags into the sous vide bath for 3 hours. When done, carefully remove the bags from the hot water and shock the bags in an ice bath for 2 minutes. Remove the crabs from the bags and pat dry.

3. To finish, preheat the oven broiler to high. Broil the crabs for 3 to 5 minutes. Once done, drizzle with the olive oil, season with salt and pepper to taste, and serve with the lemon wedges.

PREP TIP   Soft-shell crabs are also great when you finish them on a hot grill for 3 to 5 minutes.

BACON-WRAPPED SCALLOPS

Serves 4 to 6   Prep time: 5 minutes | Cook time: 30 minutes | Finishing time: 5 minutes

Warning: Highly addictive bacon-wrapped food ahead! Considered "the candy of the sea," scallops are a great choice for sous vide cooking because traditional cooking methods often leave scallops overcooked. The salty addition of bacon to naturally sweet scallops provides that sweet and salty flavor profile everyone loves. You'll probably want to double this recipe. This recipe makes a great appetizer for parties.

20 jumbo (about 1½-inch diameter) scallops

1 tablespoon diced shallots

½ teaspoon salt

½ teaspoon freshly ground black pepper

10 bacon slices, halved

2 tablespoons cold unsalted butter, cubed

1 tablespoon diced fresh chives

1. Preheat the sous vide machine to 123°F.

2. In a bowl, toss the scallops with the shallots, salt, and pepper. Wrap each scallop with bacon and secure with a toothpick. Vacuum seal the scallops with the butter cubes in a flat layer and drop the bag into the sous vide bath for 30 minutes. When done, carefully remove the bag from the hot water and shock the bag in an ice bath for 2 minutes. Remove the scallops from the bag and pat dry.

3. To finish, preheat the oven broiler to high. Broil the bacon-wrapped scallops for 2 to 4 minutes until the bacon crisps and the scallops are golden brown. Sprinkle with the chives and serve.

COD WITH OLIVE BUTTER

Serves 4   Prep time: 5 minutes | Cook time: 30 minutes | Finishing time: 5 minutes

This Mediterranean dish is packed with flavor. The olive butter is a lovely, salty spread to enjoy on meaty, flaky fish and is used in the finishing step. If I'm feeling fancy, I'll pipe this butter into little swirls (like the frosting on a cupcake) on parchment paper and then freeze it, so there are pretty little pats of butter to serve on the fish.

4 cod fillets

½ teaspoon salt

1 tablespoon finely chopped fresh thyme

2 tablespoons cold unsalted butter, cubed

1 lemon, cut into wedges

2 tablespoons Olive Butter (page 150), divided

1. Preheat the sous vide machine to 130°F.

2. Season the cod with the salt and thyme. Vacuum seal the cod with the butter cubes in a flat layer and drop the bag into the sous vide bath for 30 minutes. When done, carefully remove the bag from the hot water and shock the bag in an ice bath for 2 minutes. Using a spatula, gently remove the cod from the bag and pat dry.

3. To finish, in a large sauté pan or skillet over medium-high heat, melt 1 tablespoon of Olive Butter. Add the cod and sear for 30 to 60 seconds until lightly browned. Plate and serve each fillet with a pat of the remaining olive butter on top.

CHAPTER FIVE

find recipe on page 89

POULTRY

Poultry is easy to cook from frozen, which makes it a great choice to prepare at short notice. One little trick I have is buying chicken or turkey legs in bulk, seasoning them with fresh herbs, vacuum sealing them in dinner portions, and popping them in the freezer. When it's time to prepare them, I just add 60 minutes to the cook time.

Keep in mind that poultry can look a little funny when it comes out of the sous vide bath. Someone in my family once tossed out cooked chicken breast without trying it because they didn't think it "looked right." I set them straight, and I'll tell you the same thing: Poultry absolutely must be finished on the grill, under the broiler, or in a cast iron pan to achieve a mouth-watering presentation—and to add one last dose of immense flavor. This means the out-side of the breast or skin will be a beautiful golden brown by the time it hits the plate.

In this chapter, you'll learn the basics for cooking white and dark poultry. But you'll also learn how to make really interesting lunch sandwiches, poultry burgers, flavor-packed meatballs, and salads. And you'll have a few ideas for game day, including fried chicken and sensational wings.

POULTRY

BUFFALO CHICKEN WRAPS WITH BLUE CHEESE SLAW

Serves 4 | Prep time: 5 minutes | Cook time: 60 minutes | Finishing time: 15 minutes

A game-day favorite in my house, these Buffalo chicken wraps are spicy and crunchy. We usually eat them hot, but they are also tasty when chilled. They are perfect to take on a day-trip picnic to local vineyards or pack for a work lunch. The blue cheese slaw is something special. It's a refreshing crunchy complement to the juicy, tender pulled chicken breast. Make these wraps as spicy or mild as you'd like.

3 boneless, skinless chicken breasts

½ teaspoon garlic salt

½ teaspoon freshly ground black pepper

½ tablespoon olive oil

4 (10-inch) flour tortilla wraps

⅔ cup store-bought Buffalo sauce

1 cup Blue Cheese Slaw (page 151)

1. Preheat the sous vide machine to 140°F.

2. Season the chicken breasts with the garlic salt and pepper. Vacuum seal the chicken in a flat layer and drop the bag into the sous vide bath for 60 minutes. When done, carefully remove the bag from the hot water and shock the bag in an ice bath for 2 minutes. Remove the chicken from the bag and pat dry.

3. To finish, in a medium cast iron skillet over medium-high heat, heat the olive oil until it is shimmering. Add the chicken and sear for about 45 seconds on each side until browned. Dice the chicken and place it in a large bowl with the Buffalo sauce.

4. Assemble the wraps with the diced Buffalo chicken topped with the blue cheese slaw. To keep the wraps together, secure them with toothpicks.

MAKE IT EASY If you're making these wraps for a crowd, you can set up a DIY Buffalo chicken wrap bar. Add diced tomatoes, cotija cheese, cilantro, and diced celery.

HOLIDAY-READY HERBY TURKEY BREAST

Serves 4   Prep time: 10 minutes | Cook time: 3 hours | Finishing time: 35 minutes

One year we had a cozy Thanksgiving for two and prepared this sous vide turkey breast. We prepared it on the bone for the additional flavor and were so pleased with the results. This recipe turns out juicy, tender, and savory. And there's just no chance of a sous vide turkey drying out. On top of nailing the texture, the flavor is bright and herby. The skin gets nice and crispy after the final step under the broiler.

2 tablespoons garlic salt

1 tablespoon freshly ground black pepper

½ cup ghee (or unsalted butter)

3 tablespoons diced shallot

1 tablespoon diced fresh rosemary

1 tablespoon diced fresh thyme

2 bone-in, skin-on turkey breast halves (3 to 4 pounds total)

1 lemon, sliced

1. Preheat the sous vide machine to 145°F.

2. In a small bowl, combine the garlic salt, pepper, ghee, shallot, rosemary, and thyme to form a paste that sticks to the spoon.

3. Season the outside of the turkey breast with half the prepared paste. Vacuum seal the turkey breast with the lemon slices and drop the bag into the sous vide bath for 3 hours. When done, remove the bag from the hot water and shock the bag in an ice bath for 10 minutes. Remove the turkey from the bag and pat dry.

4. To finish, preheat the oven broiler to high. Coat the turkey with the remaining seasoning paste. Broil the turkey for 3 to 8 minutes until golden brown. Let rest for 15 minutes before serving.

STORAGE TIP Store the turkey breast in an airtight container for up to 4 days.

SOUTHERN-STYLE FRIED BUTTERMILK CHICKEN

Serves 4   Prep time: 10 minutes | Cook time: 2 hours | Finishing time: 10 minutes

It seems an unlikely combination, but pickle juice mixed with buttermilk gives this fried chicken deep flavor. The inside of the chicken will be beautifully moist, and the outside thick and crispy from the flour and cornstarch breading. We enjoy this chicken with our favorite chipotle hot sauce. These fried chicken breasts can be finished in an air fryer, traditional fryer, or on the stove.

4 chicken breasts, pounded to a 1-inch thickness

1 tablespoon diced garlic

1 teaspoon salt

1 teaspoon freshly ground black pepper

½ cup buttermilk

1 tablespoon pickle juice (optional)

¼ cup all-purpose flour

¼ cup cornstarch

½ teaspoon salt

½ teaspoon freshly ground black pepper

1. Preheat the sous vide machine to 140°F.

2. Season the chicken with the garlic, salt, and pepper. Vacuum seal the chicken breasts in a flat layer and drop the bag into the sous vide bath for 2 hours. When done, carefully remove the bag from the hot water and shock the bag in an ice bath for 2 minutes. Remove the chicken breasts from the bag and pat dry.

3. To finish, preheat the fryer to 350°F.

4. In a medium mixing bowl, thoroughly combine the buttermilk and pickle juice (if using). Set aside.

5. In a separate medium mixing bowl, stir together the flour, cornstarch, salt, and pepper until well combined. Set aside.

6. Dunk each piece of chicken first in the buttermilk mixture and then in the flour mixture to coat.

7. Place the chicken in the fryer for 2 to 3 minutes until golden brown.

8. Once cooked, carefully remove the chicken from the fryer and move to a paper towel–lined plate to dry. Serve warm.

PREP TIP To pound chicken thin, place a piece of chicken between two pieces of plastic wrap and use a rolling pin.

HONEY-CRANBERRY BARBECUE TURKEY LEG

Serves 4   Prep time: 5 minutes | Cook time: 4 hours | Finishing time: 35 minutes

When the butcher case is full of turkey legs for the holiday season, I like to stock up. I prep the meat ahead and freeze the turkey legs in their vacuum-sealed bags, already seasoned, so they're ready to thaw overnight and cook when the craving hits during the dark months of a Pacific Northwest winter. If you're serving turkey for Thanksgiving, this is a great recipe because you can buy a few extra turkey legs so multiple guests can enjoy the dark meat. The Honey-Cranberry Barbecue Sauce on these turkey legs is the perfect holiday spin on traditional sauce.

4 turkey legs

2 teaspoons smoked salt

2 teaspoons freshly ground black pepper

½ cup Honey-Cranberry Barbecue Sauce (page 152), divided

1. Preheat the sous vide machine to 155°F.

2. Season the turkey legs with the smoked salt and pepper. Vacuum seal the turkey legs in a flat layer and drop the bag into the sous vide bath for 4 hours. When done, carefully remove the bag from the hot water and shock the bag in an ice bath for 10 minutes. Remove the turkey legs from the bag and pat dry.

3. To finish, preheat the oven broiler to high.

4. Brush the turkey legs with ¼ cup of Honey-Cranberry Barbecue Sauce. Broil for 3 to 8 minutes until the skin becomes crispy. Let rest for 15 minutes before serving.

5. Plate and serve with a drizzle with the remaining ¼ cup of barbecue sauce.

MAKE IT EASY Store barbecue sauce in the refrigerator for up to 5 days. It makes a great protein marinade.

ITALIAN CHICKEN MEATBALLS

12 meatballs   Prep time: 10 minutes | Cook time: 3 hours | Finishing time: 10 minutes

Sous vide meets Italian comfort food in this dish. Meatballs are a favorite in my house, from weeknight dinners over pasta to game-day sandwiches. These chicken meatballs are breaded and spiced with tasty Italian herbs, cooked in a sous vide bath, and finished in a cast iron skillet. Top them with your favorite marinara sauce and serve over pasta. We make the meatballs from scratch, in bulk and freeze them in vacuum-sealed bags, but you could also buy frozen meatballs for this recipe.

1 pound ground chicken

⅓ cup bread crumbs

2 eggs

3 tablespoons olive oil, divided

¼ cup diced onion

¼ cup diced red bell pepper

½ teaspoon dried parsley

½ teaspoon dried oregano

1 tablespoon diced garlic

1 teaspoon salt

½ teaspoon freshly ground black pepper

½ teaspoon red pepper flakes

1. Preheat the sous vide machine to 140°F.
2. In a large mixing bowl, combine the ground chicken, bread crumbs, eggs, 2 tablespoons olive oil, onion, bell pepper, parsley, oregano, garlic, salt, pepper, and red pepper flakes. Mix until thoroughly combined.
3. Use an ice cream scoop to form 3-inch meatballs. Vacuum seal the meatballs in a flat layer and drop the bag into the sous vide bath for 3 hours. When done, carefully remove the bag from the hot water and shock the bag in an ice bath for 5 minutes. Remove the meatballs from the bag and pat dry.
4. To finish, in a medium cast iron skillet over medium-high heat, heat the remaining olive oil until it is shimmering. Add the meatballs and sear, rotating them, for 30 to 60 seconds until completely brown.
5. Plate and serve with a classic red marinara sauce.

PREP TIP Add 60 minutes to the sous vide cooking time if cooking meatballs from frozen.

GAME-DAY BUFFALO CHICKEN WINGS

Serves 4   Prep time: 10 minutes | Cook time: 1 hour | Finishing time: 10 minutes

Start the party with these juicy and crispy chicken wings! This is one of the easiest sous vide appetizers to feed a football party or barbecue. Wings cook in about an hour and are super easy to prep ahead. The skin gets crispy, whereas the inside of the chicken wings remains tender from the sous vide bath. Depending on the time of year, we finish these under the broiler, on the grill, or in the air fryer.

2 pounds chicken wings

1 cup diced red onion

¼ teaspoon salt

¼ teaspoon freshly ground black pepper

1 cup store-bought Buffalo sauce, divided

1 tablespoon chopped fresh cilantro

2 celery stalks, cut into 3-inch pieces

2 carrots, cut into 3-inch sticks

1 cup store-bought blue cheese dressing

1. Preheat the sous vide machine to 145°F.

2. In a bowl, mix together the chicken wings, onion, salt, pepper, and ¼ cup of Buffalo sauce. Vacuum seal the wings in a flat layer and drop the bag into the sous vide bath for 1 hour. When done, carefully remove the bag from the hot water and shock the bag in an ice bath for 2 minutes. Remove the wings from the bag and pat dry.

3. To finish, preheat the oven broiler to high. Line a baking sheet with parchment paper.

4. Place the wings on the prepared baking sheet and drizzle them with the remaining ¾ cup of Buffalo sauce. Broil for 3 to 5 minutes until the wings are crispy.

5. Plate the wings, sprinkle them with the cilantro, and serve with the celery, carrots, and blue cheese dressing.

PREP TIP For super crispy wings, it's very important to completely dry the chicken wings with paper towels after the sous vide bath.

PROSCIUTTO-WRAPPED CHICKEN TENDERS

Serves 4 Prep time: 10 minutes | Cook time: 1 hour | Finishing time: 10 minutes

In this recipe, thinly sliced prosciutto melts into chicken tenders, which will then melt in your mouth. I first made this recipe to use up a stash of prosciutto and fresh herbs. After some testing, I developed an olive oil marinade with fresh thyme and garlic that tastes just wonderful with salty prosciutto. All the flavors meld together during the sous vide process, and the result is a salty, rich flavor that is out of this world.

12 (1½-inch-thick)
  chicken tenders

2 tablespoons olive oil

2 tablespoons diced
  fresh thyme

1 tablespoon
  minced garlic

½ teaspoon salt

½ teaspoon freshly
  ground black pepper

12 prosciutto slices

1. Preheat the sous vide machine to 140°F.

2. Pat the chicken tenders dry. In a small mixing bowl, mix together the olive oil, thyme, garlic, salt, and pepper. Coat the chicken with the mixture. Wrap each chicken tender with a slice of prosciutto.

3. Vacuum seal the chicken in a flat layer, with space between each chicken piece, and drop the bag into the sous vide bath for 1 hour. When done, carefully remove the bag from the hot water and shock the bag in an ice bath for 2 minutes. Remove the chicken from the bag and pat dry.

4. To finish, preheat the oven broiler to high. Line a baking sheet with parchment paper.

5. Arrange the prosciutto-wrapped chicken on the prepared baking sheet and broil for 3 to 5 minutes, making sure the parchment paper doesn't burn. When the prosciutto is crispy, the chicken tenders are done.

CREAMY CHIPOTLE CHICKEN SANDWICHES

Serves 4   Prep time: 5 minutes | Cook time: 1 hour | Finishing time: 10 minutes

You just can't go wrong with a spicy chicken sandwich. It's guaranteed to hit the spot, every single time. This recipe makes a meal out of sous vide chicken breast thanks to the chipotle sauce. It's so good you might want to make a double batch to slather this sauce on everything you eat for the next few days.

4 chicken breasts, pounded to an even 1 inch thickness

½ teaspoon salt

1 tablespoon diced shallots

1 tablespoon olive oil

4 sesame buns

¼ cup Creamy Chipotle Sauce (page 153)

½ red onion, thinly sliced

¼ cup cotija cheese

1. Preheat the sous vide machine to 140°F.

2. Season the chicken with the salt and shallots. Vacuum seal the chicken in a flat layer and drop the bag into the sous vide bath for 60 minutes. When done, carefully remove the bag from the hot water and shock the bag in an ice bath for 2 minutes. Remove the chicken from the bag and pat dry.

3. To finish, in a medium cast iron skillet over medium-high heat, heat the olive oil until it is shimmering. Add the chicken and sear each side for 30 to 45 seconds until browned.

4. Plate the sandwiches by placing chicken on the bottom of each sesame bun. Top with the chipotle sauce, red onion, and cotija cheese.

SUBSTITUTION TIP You can use queso fresco instead of cotija cheese.

GRILLED CHICKEN BREAST WITH LEMON-HONEY-PEPPER GLAZE

Serves 4 | Prep time: 5 minutes | Cook time: 1 hour | Finishing time: 10 minutes

Summer entertaining is easy with the sous vide machine. The chicken can be cooked up to 24 hours ahead of time, and the glaze can be made ahead, too. When guests arrive, all you have to do is fire up the grill to finish the chicken with the Lemon-Honey-Pepper Glaze, then serve. Offer your guests a choice of sandwich rolls and salad greens to serve themselves.

4 chicken breasts

2 teaspoons smoked salt

1 teaspoon freshly ground black pepper

4 lemon slices

½ cup Lemon-Honey-Pepper Glaze (page 145), divided

1. Preheat the sous vide machine to 140°F.

2. Season the chicken with the salt and pepper. Vacuum seal the chicken in a flat layer with a slice of lemon on each piece, and drop the bag into the sous vide bath for 1 hour. When done, carefully remove the bag from the hot water and shock the bag in an ice bath for 2 minutes. Remove the chicken from the bag and pat dry.

3. To finish, preheat the grill to high. Brush the chicken with ¼ cup of Lemon-Honey-Pepper Glaze and grill the chicken for 1 to 2 minutes on each side until browned.

4. Plate and serve drizzled with the remaining ¼ cup of glaze.

MAKE IT EASY Leftovers are great for chilled chicken salads the next day. Whisk leftover glaze with a little more vinegar, olive oil, salt, and pepper to make a dressing.

CURRY-SPICED CHICKEN THIGHS

Serves 4   Prep time: 5 minutes | Cook time: 4 hours | Finishing time: 15 minutes

Chicken thighs are one of our go-to meals during a busy week. We keep our pantry stocked with a variety of spices, so it's easy to change up the flavors. One of the really good parts of these thighs is their crispy, flavorful skin, created thanks to the seasoned olive oil that is brushed on the chicken before it broils. We serve these Indian-inspired chicken thighs on top of salads, saffron rice, or potatoes.

FOR THE CHICKEN THIGHS

4 bone-in, skin-on
   chicken thighs

1 teaspoon salt

1 teaspoon freshly
   ground black pepper

¼ teaspoon
   ground cumin

¼ teaspoon
   smoked paprika

1 tablespoon finely
   chopped fresh
   oregano, divided

FOR THE CURRY-SPICED OLIVE OIL

½ tablespoon turmeric

1 teaspoon ground cumin

1 teaspoon
   ground coriander

1 teaspoon
   smoked paprika

½ teaspoon dry mustard

¼ teaspoon cinnamon

1 tablespoon olive oil

TO SOUS VIDE AND FINISH THE CHICKEN THIGHS

1. Preheat the sous vide machine to 140°F.

2. Season the chicken thighs with the salt, pepper, cumin, paprika, and ½ tablespoon of oregano. Vacuum seal the chicken thighs in a flat layer and drop the bag into the sous vide bath for 4 hours. When done, carefully remove the bag from the hot water and shock the bag in an ice bath for 2 minutes. Remove the chicken thighs from the bag and pat dry.

3. To finish, preheat the oven broiler to high. Line a baking sheet with parchment paper.

4. Arrange the chicken thighs on the prepared baking sheet and brush the curry spice olive oil on top. Broil the chicken thighs for 3 to 5 minutes until the skin is crispy, making sure the parchment paper doesn't burn.

5. Plate and serve sprinkled with the remaining ½ tablespoon of fresh oregano.

TO MAKE THE CURRY-SPICED OLIVE OIL

While the chicken thighs cook, in a small bowl, make the curry spice olive oil by mixing together the turmeric, cumin, coriander, paprika, mustard, and cinnamon. Add the olive oil and whisk together. Set aside.

CRANBERRY-TURKEY MEATBALLS

About 12 meatballs   Prep time: 10 minutes | Cook time: 3 hours | Finishing time: 10 minutes

Each bite of these meatballs is like an entire Thanksgiving meal. They are both sweet from the cranberries and savory from the herbs. Make these year-round to get all those holiday feels throughout the year. Or throw them together for a holiday potluck or party for a festive but easy main dish.

FOR THE MEATBALLS

1 pound ground turkey

⅔ cup dried cranberries, diced

1 egg

¼ cup diced onion

1 teaspoon diced garlic

½ cup peeled and shredded Granny Smith apple

1 teaspoon freshly squeezed lemon juice

⅓ cup bread crumbs

1 teaspoon dried sage

2 tablespoons finely chopped fresh parsley, divided

½ teaspoon salt

¼ teaspoon freshly ground black pepper

1 tablespoon olive oil

FOR THE CRANBERRY BARBECUE SAUCE

1 cup jellied cranberry sauce

1 cup barbecue sauce

½ teaspoon freshly ground black pepper

TO SOUS VIDE AND FINISH THE MEATBALLS

1. Preheat the sous vide machine to 140°F.

2. In a large mixing bowl, combine the ground turkey, cranberries, egg, onion, garlic, apple, lemon juice, bread crumbs, sage, 1 tablespoon of parsley, salt, and pepper and mix until well combined. Use an ice cream scoop to form 3-inch meatballs.

3. Vacuum seal the meatballs in a flat layer and drop the bag into the sous vide bath for 3 hours. When done, carefully remove the bag from the hot water and shock the bag in an ice bath for 5 minutes. Remove the meatballs from the bag and pat dry. Set aside.

4. To finish, in a medium cast iron skillet over medium-high heat, heat the olive oil until it is shimmering. Add the meatballs and sear them, rotating each, for 30 to 60 seconds until completely seared.

5. Plate and serve with the prepared cranberry barbecue sauce and a sprinkle of the remaining parsley.

TO MAKE THE CRANBERRY BARBECUE SAUCE

In a small saucepan over medium-low heat, simmer the cranberry sauce, barbecue sauce, and pepper for 10 minutes, whisking regularly. Set aside.

MAKE IT EASY   Any leftover sauce makes a delicious protein marinade for another day.

SWEET HONEY-SRIRACHA CHICKEN WINGS

Serves 4 | Prep time: 5 minutes | Cook time: 1 hour | Finishing time: 10 minutes

If you want to make mouths water before anyone even sees the food . . . serve these! The ingredients fill the air with that sweet-and-sour aroma that gets people off the couch and into the kitchen to see what smells so good. Sous vide chicken wings are one of my favorite ways to show off this special little gadget to a crowd. They come together quickly, and you can buy the wings inexpensively in bulk. I love serving these wings with sesame seeds and chopped scallions. The contrast of the sticky orange-red wings against the bright-green garnish makes this a photo-worthy dish.

2 pounds chicken wings

1 teaspoon salt

1 teaspoon freshly ground black pepper

½ cup Sweet Honey-Sriracha Sauce (page 154)

1 tablespoon sesame seeds (optional)

3 scallions, green parts only, diced

1. Preheat the sous vide machine to 145°F.

2. Season the chicken wings with the salt and pepper. Vacuum seal the chicken wings in a single layer with a half-inch space between each wing. Use multiple vacuum seal bags, if needed, to allow all the wings to be fully submerged when in the sous vide bath. Sous vide the chicken wings for 1 hour. When done, carefully remove the bag(s) from the hot water. Remove the wings from the bag, place them on a paper towel–lined cutting board, and pat dry.

3. To finish, preheat the oven broiler to high. Line a large rimmed baking sheet with parchment paper.

4. In a large mixing bowl, combine the Sweet Honey-Sriracha sauce and the wings. Toss until well coated, then arrange the wings on the prepared baking sheet.

5. Broil the wings for 2 to 4 minutes until the sauce sets. Keep an eye on the parchment paper so it doesn't burn.

6. Garnish the wings with the sesame seeds and diced scallions.

MAKE IT EASY Prepare the sauce and cook the wings in the sous vide machine up to a day in advance. Mix the wings with the sauce when it's time to broil and serve them.

BLACKENED CHICKEN SALAD

Serves 4 | Prep time: 5 minutes | Cook time: 1 hour | Finishing time: 15 minutes

This recipe is one of the easiest sous-vide-ahead lunches you'll come across, while being a delicious twist on typical chicken salad. It's packed with vegetables and is chilled in the refrigerator, ready to make weekday lunches or picnics taste great. Serve this blackened chicken salad on wraps or sandwich rolls, or keep it on the lighter side by serving with lettuce cups.

FOR THE BLACKENED CHICKEN

4 boneless, skinless
  chicken breasts

1 teaspoon diced garlic

½ teaspoon salt

½ teaspoon freshly
  ground black pepper

½ tablespoon olive oil

FOR THE CHICKEN SALAD

½ cup shredded carrots

¼ cup diced red onion

¼ cup sour cream

¼ cup Greek yogurt

1 tablespoon olive oil

Salt

Freshly ground
  black pepper

1 tablespoon diced
  fresh parsley

TO SOUS VIDE AND FINISH THE BLACKENED CHICKEN

1. Preheat the sous vide machine to 140°F.
2. Season the chicken breasts with the garlic, salt, and pepper.
3. Vacuum seal the chicken in a flat layer and drop the bag into the sous vide bath for 60 minutes. When done, carefully remove the bag from the hot water and shock the bag in an ice bath for 2 minutes. Remove the chicken from the bag and pat dry.
4. To finish, in a medium cast iron skillet over medium-high heat, heat the olive oil. Add the chicken to the skillet and sear for about 45 seconds on each side until browned. Dice the chicken.

TO MAKE THE SALAD

In a large serving bowl, combine all the carrots, onion, sour cream, yogurt, olive oil, salt, pepper, and parsley. Add the diced blackened chicken and toss to combine.

POMEGRANATE-GLAZED CHICKEN LEGS

Serves 4   Prep time: 5 minutes | Cook time: 3 hours | Finishing time: 10 minutes

Pomegranate molasses is a star ingredient in this dish. This recipe is both sweet and savory, with the skin of the chicken legs getting crispy with the pomegranate glaze in the final step. Serve with a side of tabbouleh or hummus.

8 skin-on chicken legs

½ teaspoon salt

½ teaspoon freshly ground black pepper

¼ cup Pomegranate Glaze (page 155)

2 teaspoons chopped fresh parsley

1. Preheat the sous vide machine to 140°F.

2. Season the chicken legs with the salt and pepper. Vacuum seal the chicken legs in a flat layer and drop the bag into the sous vide bath for 3 hours. When done, carefully remove the bag from the hot water and shock the bag in an ice bath for 2 minutes. Remove the chicken legs from the bag and pat dry.

3. To finish, preheat the oven broiler to high. Line a baking sheet with parchment paper.

4. Arrange the chicken legs on the prepared baking sheet. Brush the chicken legs with the Pomegranate Glaze and broil for 3 to 5 minutes until the skin is crispy, making sure the parchment paper doesn't burn.

5. Plate and serve sprinkled with the parsley.

TURKEY, APPLE, AND BRIE SANDWICH

Serves 4   Prep time: 5 minutes | Cook time: 3 hours | Finishing time: 20 minutes

This recipe makes a generous serving of turkey to enjoy in sandwiches all week. The juicy and tender turkey also holds up in the refrigerator for a couple of days. During the holiday season, I replace the apples with leftover cranberry sauce to switch up the flavors. It's best to work with extremely fresh French bread for this recipe. The combo of Brie and apple is fantastic, especially when topped with the balsamic honey dressing.

FOR THE TURKEY BREAST

1 pound boneless
turkey breast

1 packet ranch
seasoning mix

½ tablespoon olive oil

FOR THE DRESSING

1½ tablespoons
balsamic vinegar

1 teaspoon honey

½ tablespoon olive oil

⅛ teaspoon salt

⅛ teaspoon freshly
ground black pepper

FOR THE SANDWICHES

4 (6-inch) French
baguette rolls

1 Gala apple, thinly sliced

8 ounces Brie cheese,
thinly sliced

1½ cups arugula

TO SOUS VIDE AND FINISH THE TURKEY BREAST

1. Preheat the sous vide machine to 140°F.
2. Season the turkey with the ranch seasoning. Vacuum seal the turkey breast in a flat layer and drop the bag into the sous vide bath for 3 hours. When done, carefully remove the bag from the hot water and shock the bag in an ice bath for 2 minutes. Remove the turkey breast from the bag and pat dry.
3. To finish, preheat the oven broiler to high. Line a baking sheet with parchment paper.
4. Brush the turkey with the olive oil and broil for 5 minutes until the skin is crispy, making sure the parchment paper doesn't burn. Once done, let the turkey cool for 10 minutes, then slice it thinly. Set aside.

TO MAKE THE DRESSING

In a small mixing bowl, whisk together the balsamic vinegar, honey, olive oil, salt, and pepper until well combined.

TO ASSEMBLE THE SANDWICHES

On each French baguette, layer sliced turkey, Gala apple slices, Brie slices, and arugula. Drizzle with the prepared dressing and enjoy.

DUCK CONFIT WITH ORANGE SAUCE

Serves 4 | Prep time: 5 minutes | Cook time: 12 hours | Finishing time: 10 minutes

I fell in love with duck confit in Portland while filming a behind-the-scenes online series with chefs at their restaurants. In one episode, I featured a French chef who prepared duck confit the traditional way. It was spectacular, but I don't work in a traditional French kitchen, so to emulate that tasty dish at home, I use my sous vide machine. This recipe cooks duck legs perfectly tender without drying them out. The addition of the orange sauce is a wonderful complement to the duck because citrus flavors are delicious with poultry. If time allows, refrigerate the duck in the salt, rosemary, and duck fat for up to a day ahead.

FOR THE DUCK LEGS

8 duck legs

1 tablespoon salt

1 tablespoon finely chopped fresh rosemary

1 cup duck fat

1 tablespoon cold unsalted butter

FOR THE ORANGE SAUCE

½ tablespoon cornstarch

1 tablespoon water

1 cup orange juice

3 tablespoons honey

½ teaspoon dried parsley

1 tablespoon Dijon mustard

½ teaspoon garlic salt

¼ teaspoon freshly ground black pepper

TO SOUS VIDE AND FINISH THE DUCK LEGS

1. Preheat the sous vide machine to 168°F.
2. Rub the duck legs with the salt, rosemary, and duck fat. Vacuum seal the duck legs in a flat layer and drop the bag into the sous vide bath for 12 hours. When done, carefully remove the bag from the hot water and shock the bag in an ice bath for 2 minutes. Remove the duck from the bag and pat dry. Set aside.
3. In a medium cast iron skillet over medium-high heat, melt the butter. While the pan heats, brush the duck legs with some orange sauce. Add the duck legs to the skillet and sear for 45 to 60 seconds on each side until crispy and brown.
4. Plate and drizzle with the remaining orange sauce.

TO MAKE THE ORANGE SAUCE

In a small saucepan over medium heat, mix together the cornstarch and water. Add the orange juice, honey, parsley, mustard, garlic salt, and pepper. Whisk until combined, about 5 minutes. Remove from the heat. Set aside.

INGREDIENT TIP Duck fat is a pretty easy ingredient to get your hands on. If it's not available at a store near you, check online.

CHICKEN THIGHS WITH LEMON-TAHINI SAUCE

Serves 4 | Prep time: 5 minutes | Cook time: 4 hours | Finishing time: 10 minutes

Lemon and chicken were made for each other. This recipe leans on one of my favorite kitchen staples: tahini paste, which is available everywhere these days. The dressing is addictive, and I love plating these juicy but crispy sous vide chicken thighs over a bed of greens or couscous so I can enjoy every last drop of the sauce.

8 skin-on, bone-in chicken thighs

1 teaspoon garlic salt

¼ teaspoon freshly ground black pepper

1½ tablespoons chopped parsley, divided

½ lemon, sliced

½ tablespoon olive oil

¼ cup Lemon-Tahini Sauce (page 148)

1. Preheat the sous vide machine to 140°F.

2. Season the chicken thighs with the garlic salt and pepper. Vacuum seal the chicken thighs topped with ½ tablespoon of parsley and the lemon slices in a flat layer. Drop the bag into the sous vide bath for 4 hours. When done, carefully remove the bag from the hot water and shock the bag in an ice bath for 2 minutes. Remove the chicken thighs from the bag and pat dry.

3. To finish, in a medium cast iron skillet over medium-high heat, heat the olive oil until it is shimmering. Add the chicken thighs and sear for 30 to 60 seconds until brown and crispy. Plate and serve with a large spoonful of Lemon-Tahini Sauce and sprinkle the remaining parsley on top.

GREEK TURKEY BURGER

Serves 4   Prep time: 10 minutes | Cook time: 1 hour, 30 minutes | Finishing time: 15 minutes

Making turkey burgers at home used to be extremely hit-or-miss because they can easily dry out due to their lack of fat. But sous vide cooking makes them a safe bet for enjoying at home. The juices of the turkey aren't lost to heat but are reabsorbed right into these burgers in the vacuum-sealed bag. This version contains Greek flavors and is topped with creamy, salty feta cheese.

1½ pounds ground turkey

⅓ cup finely diced onion

1 tablespoon pitted and diced Kalamata olives

1 tablespoon finely chopped fresh parsley

1 tablespoon finely chopped fresh dill, plus 2 teaspoons

1 tablespoon diced garlic

½ teaspoon smoked paprika

¼ teaspoon dried thyme

¼ teaspoon ground nutmeg

1 tablespoon cold unsalted butter

4 seeded hamburger buns

4 slices tomato

1 cup feta cheese, from brine, thinly sliced

2 teaspoons chopped fresh dill

1. Preheat the sous vide machine to 145°F.

2. In a medium mixing bowl, combine the turkey, onion, olives, parsley, 1 tablespoon of dill, the garlic, paprika, thyme, and nutmeg. Mix until thoroughly combined.

3. Form four patties, each about 1½ inches thick. Vacuum seal the turkey burgers in a flat layer and drop the bag into the sous vide bath for 90 minutes. When done, carefully remove the bag from the hot water and shock the bag in an ice bath for 5 minutes. Remove the turkey burgers from the bag and pat dry.

4. To finish, in a medium cast iron skillet over medium-high heat, melt the butter. Add the burgers and sear for 30 to 60 seconds on each side until a browned crust forms.

5. Plate each burger by topping each bun base with a turkey burger, a slice of tomato, one-quarter of the feta cheese, and ½ teaspoon of dill. Place the bun tops on top, and serve.

SUBSTITUTION TIP These burgers are also delicious topped with tzatziki sauce.

CHAPTER SIX

find recipe on page 105

PORK

All the risk in cooking pork loins and chops at home dissolve when cooking them sous vide style. The pork cooks perfectly edge to edge; it never overcooks. The sous vide cooking method helps inject and retain flavor in the pork, which otherwise can be light on flavor. The pork juices pump back into the meat as it cooks, and herbs and seasonings leave their tasty mark.

Beyond loins and chops, there's a ton of other pork options to experiment with and to enjoy. If you thought it would be impossible to love bacon any more than you already do, get ready to be surprised. Bacon cooked for 8 hours in a sous vide bath is nothing short of spectacular. It turns out meaty and doesn't shrink down. All the delicious flavors stay right there in the bacon instead of leaching out as grease.

Ribs, sausage, and pork belly are other wonderful main dish pork cuts to try. In this chapter, you'll learn all about how to season, prepare, and serve them with flavorful sauces.

PORK

TAILGATE-READY SAUSAGE, PEPPERS, AND ONION SANDWICH

Serves 4   Prep time: 15 minutes | Cook time: 2 hours | Finishing time: 10 minutes

Having a tasty recipe for sausage sandwiches is essential for feeding a game-day crowd. These sandwiches are loaded with Dijon mustard, onions, and peppers and are served with provolone cheese on soft hoagie rolls. Since the onions and peppers technically need to sous vide at a higher temperature than sausage (to break down), they are quickly sautéed on the stovetop before adding them to the sous vide bag. The flavors of the veggies mingle beautifully with the sausage and—get this—it's all cooked in beer!

½ tablespoon olive oil

1 medium yellow onion, halved, then thinly sliced

1 medium red bell pepper, thinly sliced

1 teaspoon diced garlic

¼ teaspoon salt

¼ teaspoon freshly ground black pepper

1 cup lager beer

4 cooked Italian sausages

4 hoagie rolls

4 tablespoons Dijon mustard

8 slices provolone cheese

1. Preheat the sous vide machine to 140°F.

2. In a medium saucepan over medium heat, heat the olive oil for 1 minute. Add the onion, bell pepper, and garlic. Season with the salt and pepper and stir regularly for 5 minutes. Pour the beer into the pan and reduce the heat to medium-low. Simmer for 5 minutes, then transfer the mixture to a sous vide bag. Add the sausages to the bag and seal. Because of all the liquid, the water displacement method (see page 10) may be preferable to vacuum sealing the ingredients.

3. Drop the bag into the sous vide bath for 2 hours. When done, carefully remove the bag from the hot water. Transfer all the ingredients in the bag to a medium saucepan over medium heat and cook, stirring regularly, until any juices cook off. Set aside.

4. To finish, toast the hoagie rolls, if you like, then smear each side of the rolls with the Dijon mustard. Add the sausages, onions, peppers, and provolone cheese and serve.

SUBSTITUTION TIP Substitute chicken or vegetable broth for the beer.

PORK SHOULDER AND PINEAPPLE QUESADILLAS

Serves 4   Prep time: 15 minutes | Cook time: 48 hours | Finishing time: 10 minutes

This recipe starts with a basic sous vide pork shoulder recipe and turns it into a sweet- and savory-pineapple quesadilla. The pork is seared before going into the bag and comes out with a beautiful bark and a tender, fall-apart inside. The pork doesn't require much hands-on time, but it is one of the longer sous vide baths at about two days of cook time. Remember to check regularly and replenish the water level of the bath if needed.

3 pounds pork shoulder

3 tablespoons
  barbecue salt

1 tablespoon freshly
  ground black pepper

2 tablespoons olive oil

3 cups shredded
  Cheddar cheese

1 8-ounce can crushed
  pineapples, strained

1 tablespoon finely
  chopped fresh cilantro

Hot sauce

8 (10-inch) flour tortillas

4 tablespoons
  (½ stick) cold unsalted
  butter divided

Guacamole (optional)

Sour cream (optional)

1. Preheat the sous vide machine to 165°F.

2. Rub the pork shoulder with the barbecue salt and pepper.

3. In a large skillet over medium-high heat, heat the olive oil until it is shimmering. Add the pork shoulder and sear it on each side for 3 to 5 minutes to create a thick brown bark.

4. Vacuum seal the pork and drop the bag into the sous vide bath for 48 hours. When done, carefully remove the pork from the hot water and transfer to a cutting board. With two forks, pull apart the pork to shred it completely. Set aside.

5. To finish, place ½ cup of pulled pork and one-fourth of the cheese, crushed pineapple, cilantro, and hot sauce to taste between two tortillas. Set aside.

6. In a large skillet over medium heat, melt 1 tablespoon of butter. Add 1 quesadilla to the skillet and cook until golden brown, about 5 minutes on each side. Repeat for the remaining quesadillas.

7. Cut each quesadilla into quarters and serve with sour cream or guacamole (if using).

PREP TIP Save a little crushed pineapple to mix with mashed avocado for a tasty guacamole to serve on the side.

OMG BACON BLT

Serves 4 Prep time: 5 minutes | Cook time: 8 hours | Finishing time: 5 minutes

There's no way bacon could get any better, right? Wrong! Sous vide bacon is on a completely different level than any traditionally cooked bacon. The first time we cooked bacon this way, we couldn't believe how much of the bacon stayed intact. The presentation is great—it stays nice and flat—and the texture is chewy in a good way. After the sous vide bath, the bacon is quickly fried to get a crisp exterior. This recipe is an absolute must!

1 pound bacon

8 pieces toast

2 tablespoons mayonnaise

2 cups shredded lettuce

2 beefsteak
  tomatoes, sliced

Hot sauce (optional)

1. Preheat the sous vide machine to 142°F.

2. Transfer the bacon from its original packaging to a sous vide bag. The bacon can be arranged overlapping, the way it is in the bacon packaging.

3. Vacuum seal the bacon and drop the bag into the sous vide bath for 8 hours. When done, carefully remove the bag from the hot water. Remove the bacon from the bag and pat dry.

4. To finish, heat a large skillet over medium-high heat and add the bacon. Sear each side for 30 to 60 seconds until it gets crispy. Once done, transfer to a paper towel–lined cutting board. Set aside.

5. Spread ¼ tablespoon of mayonnaise on one side of 4 pieces of toast, then layer with the bacon slices, tomatoes, and lettuce and top with the remaining pieces of toast.

MAKE IT EASY This recipe is a great one to sous vide in a huge batch, then enjoy for days with different recipes or for breakfast. Just sear the bacon in a pan when you're ready to eat.

PULLED PORK TACOS WITH PORKY BARBECUE SAUCE

Serves 4   Prep time: 15 minutes | Cook time: 48 hours | Finishing time: 10 minutes

Sous vide cooking of the pork does two things here. First, and most obviously, it creates insanely tender pulled pork. Second, the long cook time creates taco-seasoned pork drippings that my husband always insists on turning into a porky barbecue sauce. Enjoy the pork in sandwiches the next day.

FOR THE PULLED PORK

1 tablespoon chili powder

½ tablespoon garlic salt

1 tablespoon freshly ground black pepper

½ tablespoon ground cumin

1 teaspoon red pepper flakes

3 pounds pork shoulder

2 tablespoons olive oil

FOR THE SAUCE

4 tablespoons leftover pork juice

3 tablespoons cold unsalted butter

1 tablespoon barbecue sauce

FOR THE TACOS

Mini corn/flour tortillas

2 cups frozen corn, thawed

½ cup queso fresco crumbles

1 tablespoon finely chopped fresh cilantro

1 lime, cut into wedges

TO SOUS VIDE THE PULLED PORK

1. Preheat the sous vide machine to 165°F.

2. In a small mixing bowl, combine the chili powder, garlic salt, black pepper, cumin, and red pepper flakes. Rub the pork shoulder with the seasonings. Set aside.

3. In a medium skillet over medium-high heat, heat the olive oil until it is shimmering. Add the pork shoulder and sear on each side for 3 to 5 minutes to create a thick brown bark.

4. Vacuum seal the pork and drop the bag into the sous vide bath for 48 hours. When done, carefully remove the bag from the hot water. Remove the pork from the bag and transfer to a cutting board. With two forks, pull apart the pork to shred it thoroughly. Set aside.

TO MAKE THE SAUCE AND ASSEMBLE THE TACOS

1. In a small saucepan over medium heat, combine the leftover pork juice, butter, and barbecue sauce. Stir for 5 minutes until well combined. Set aside.

2. On each mini tortilla, pile some pulled pork, corn, cheese, and cilantro. Add a drizzle of sauce and serve with a lime wedge.

PREP TIP Check the water level of the sous vide bath regularly. Long cook times often require replenishing the water.

HAM NUGGET WITH PINEAPPLE-MAPLE GLAZE

Serves 4   Prep time: 5 minutes | Cook time: 5 hours | Finishing time: 20 minutes

Making sous vide main dishes for the holidays frees up the oven for other recipes. This ham nugget is a classic, made even juicier when cooked sous vide style. Since most ham nuggets come already seasoned, you can doctor it up as much or as little as desired. In this recipe, the ham cooks in its own juices and benefits from an additional sweet layer from crushed pineapple and is balanced with a hint of spice from red pepper flakes.

1 (28-ounce) boneless ham nugget

¼ cup maple syrup

½ cup crushed pineapple

½ teaspoon red pepper flakes

1 tablespoon unsalted butter, melted

2 teaspoons honey

Mustard, for serving

1. Preheat the sous vide machine to 140°F.

2. Vacuum seal the ham, maple syrup, pineapple, and red pepper flakes and drop the bag into the sous vide bath for 5 hours. When done, carefully remove the bag from the hot water. Remove the ham from the bag and pat dry.

3. To finish, preheat the oven broiler to high. Line a baking sheet with parchment paper.

4. In a small bowl, mix the butter with the honey. Place the ham nugget on the prepared baking sheet and brush it with the glaze. Broil for 4 to 5 minutes to caramelize the outside, making sure the parchment paper doesn't burn. Let the nugget sit for 5 to 10 minutes, then carve and serve with mustard.

PREP TIP Another option for getting the maple syrup in the vacuum-sealed bag is to freeze the syrup ahead of time on a baking sheet lined with parchment paper. It will not freeze solid, but it will be easier to vacuum seal.

CUBAN PORK SANDWICH

Serves 4 | Prep time: 5 minutes | Cook time: 2 hours, 30 minutes | Finishing time: 20 minutes

This sandwich takes me back to Miami, where my husband and I enjoyed our first authentic Cuban pork sandwich the week we got engaged. My husband found a hidden gem where we could feel like locals and eat Cuban sandwiches while sitting at the kitchen bar. If you've never had one, it's basically a pork and cheese sandwich prepared in a very specific way, with pork marinated in mojo sauce, Swiss cheese, mustard, and pickles on soft rolls. Some versions add ham and salami. This is a great recipe to prepare ahead and toss in a panini press or in the oven to melt the cheese when it's time to eat.

1 (4- to 5-pound) **boneless pork loin**

¼ cup **Mojo Sauce** (page 158), **divided**

3 tablespoons **yellow mustard**

4 (8-inch) **soft rolls**

8 slices **ham** (optional)

8 slices **salami** (optional)

8 slices **Swiss cheese**

⅓ cup **dill pickles**

1. Preheat the sous vide machine to 137°F.
2. Vacuum seal the pork with 2 tablespoons of mojo sauce and drop the bag into the sous vide bath for 2 hours, 30 minutes. When done, carefully remove the bag from the hot water and shock the bag in an ice bath for 2 minutes. Remove the pork from the bag and pat dry.
3. To finish, preheat the oven broiler to high. Brush the pork with the remaining 2 tablespoons of mojo sauce and broil for about 5 minutes until browned. Let rest for 5 to 10 minutes before slicing into ½-inch-thick pieces.
4. Assemble the sandwiches by spreading the mustard on the soft rolls. To each roll, add 2 slices each of pork, ham (if using), salami (if using), Swiss cheese, and a few dill pickles. Toast the sandwiches in a panini press or in the oven, if desired. Serve hot.

MAKE IT EASY It can be easier to vacuum seal liquids when they are frozen. You can make a batch of mojo sauce in advance, freeze it in ice cube trays, and pop the sauce cubes in with the pork when it's time to sous vide.

PORK BELLY PASTA

Serves 4   Prep time: 5 minutes | Cook time: 8 hours | Finishing time: 20 minutes

This pasta delivers all the comfort-food feels. It's perfect for a Sunday night. The sous vide pork belly is tenderized to the point that it melts in your mouth. The smoked salt adds a layer of flavor that's unexpected and savory. And the creamy, cheesy egg sauce will have you licking your spoon.

2 pounds pork belly, cut into 2-inch squares

2 teaspoons smoked salt (optional)

1½ pounds fusilli pasta

1 cup frozen corn, thawed

3 large eggs

1 cup freshly grated Parmesan cheese, divided, plus more for garnish

¼ cup finely chopped fresh Italian parsley, plus more for garnish

1 tablespoon cold unsalted butter

Freshly ground black pepper

1. Preheat the sous vide machine to 170°F.

2. Season the pork belly with the smoked salt, if using. Vacuum seal the pork belly in a flat layer and drop the bag into the sous vide bath for 8 hours. When done, carefully remove the bag from the hot water, remove the pork belly from the bag, and pat dry.

3. To finish, bring a half-filled medium saucepan of water to a boil over medium-high heat. When the water begins to boil, add the fusilli pasta and continue to cook until al dente, about 7 minutes. One minute before the boiling time is complete, add the corn. Drain the pasta and corn, reserving 1 cup of the water, and set aside.

4. In a large mixing bowl, thoroughly whisk together the eggs, ½ cup of Parmesan cheese, and the parsley.

5. In a medium skillet over medium-high heat, melt the butter. Add the pork belly and sear to crisp the edges, 1 to 2 minutes. Leave it in the skillet to keep warm.

6. Add ½ cup of the reserved pasta water to the egg and cheese mixture. Whisk to combine, then stir in the fusilli pasta and pork belly. Add additional cheese to taste and 1 tablespoon at a time of additional reserved pasta water, if needed, to keep the sauce creamy.

7. Season with pepper and sprinkle with parsley.

PORK CHOPS WITH CAROLINA-STYLE YELLOW MUSTARD BARBECUE SAUCE

Serves 4   Prep time: 5 minutes | Cook time: 2 hours, 30 minutes | Finishing time: 20 minutes

This is the type of dish that can turn anyone into a pork chops lover because they never turn out dry. The tangy Carolina-Style yellow mustard barbecue sauce is pork's perfect companion. Once you try pork chops sous vide style, you'll fall in love with how tender and ridiculously juicy they are. Leftovers make delicious pork sandwiches for days to come.

4 (1½-inch-thick) boneless pork chops

2 teaspoons chopped garlic

Salt

Freshly ground black pepper

10 cilantro sprigs

1 tablespoon olive oil

2 tablespoons Carolina-Style Yellow Mustard Barbecue Sauce (page 159)

1 tablespoon finely chopped fresh chives (optional, for garnish)

1. Preheat the sous vide machine to 140°F.

2. Season the pork chops with the garlic, salt, and pepper. Vacuum seal the pork chops with the cilantro on top in a flat layer and drop the bag into the sous vide bath for 2 hours, 30 minutes. When done, carefully remove the bag from the hot water and shock the bag in an ice bath for 2 minutes. Remove the pork chops from the bag, discard the herbs, and pat dry.

3. To finish, in a medium cast iron skillet over medium-high heat, heat the olive oil until it is shimmering. Add the pork chops and sear on each side until a brown crust forms, 30 to 60 seconds. To sear the edges, use tongs to hold the pork chops. Once seared, let the chops rest on a cutting board for 5 to 10 minutes before slicing and serving.

4. Plate with a drizzle of Carolina-Style Yellow Mustard Barbecue Sauce and garnish with the chives (if using) or leftover cilantro.

PREP TIP You can spoon a little pork juice from the hot skillet over the pork chops before slicing them, to recrisp the crust and heat the pork chops.

GROUND PORK LETTUCE WRAPS

Serves 4 Prep time: 5 minutes | Cook time: 2 hours | Finishing time: 10 minutes

These lettuce cups are tasty to eat chilled for work lunches or served hot for dinner. They are like little handheld salads, packed with juicy sous vide pork. We serve them DIY style with various ingredients for each person to personalize their meal. In this recipe you'll find our favorite additions, including a sweet-and-savory soy Sriracha sauce to drizzle on top.

1½ pounds ground pork

1 tablespoon diced garlic

1 teaspoon freshly grated ginger

1 teaspoon salt

1 head butter lettuce

1 cup shredded carrots

½ cup diced red onion

2 tablespoons sesame seeds

2 tablespoons chopped scallions, green parts only

2 tablespoons Soy Sriracha Sauce (page 157)

1. Preheat the sous vide machine to 140°F.

2. Vacuum seal the ground pork, garlic, ginger, and salt in a flat layer and drop the bag into the sous vide bath for 2 hours. When done, carefully remove the bag from the hot water. Open the bag and pour the ground pork through a strainer to remove any excess liquid.

3. To finish, serve the pork DIY style with the lettuce, carrots, red onion, sesame seeds, scallions, and sauce in individual bowls.

SUBSTITUTION TIP Try other lettuces, such as Boston Bibb, iceberg, or romaine.

HERBY SAUSAGE BREAKFAST PATTIES

Serves 4   Prep time: 20 minutes | Cook time: 2 hours | Finishing time: 5 minutes

Looking for something to pair with sous vide egg cups for breakfast? These sausage patties are a perfect match. Make them ahead in bulk and freeze them so they're ready for meal-prep days.

1½ pounds ground pork

1 tablespoon diced garlic

1 tablespoon dried
  sage, crumbled

2 teaspoons dried thyme

2 teaspoons dried
  fennel, crushed

1 tablespoon brown sugar

1 teaspoon red
  pepper flakes

1 teaspoon salt

1 teaspoon freshly
  ground black pepper

1 large egg

1 tablespoon olive oil

1. Preheat the sous vide machine to 145°F.

2. In a large mixing bowl, combine the ground pork, garlic, sage, thyme, fennel, brown sugar, red pepper flakes, salt, black pepper, and egg. Mix thoroughly until well combined. Chill in the freezer for 10 minutes, then form the mixture into 3-inch sausage patties about a half-inch thick.

3. Vacuum seal the sausage patties in a flat layer and drop the bag into the sous vide bath for 2 hours. When done, carefully remove the bag from the sous vide bath, remove the patties from the bag, drain each patty of excess liquid, and pat dry.

4. To finish, in a medium cast iron skillet over medium-high heat, heat the olive oil until it is shimmering. Add the patties and sear on each side for 1 to 2 minutes until browned. Serve while hot.

SMOKY BROWN SUGAR PORK LOIN ROAST

Serves 4   Prep time: 5 minutes | Cook time: 2 hours, 30 minutes | Finishing time: 20 minutes

For the holidays, I like to serve a couple of main dish meat options. This pork loin is a wonderful main to include as it doesn't require handholding throughout the cooking process the way traditional roast pork does. The pork goes into the sous vide bath with a handful of complementary bold and sweet flavors, including brown sugar, rosemary, and garlic salt. In the final step, the loin is seared to create a beautiful crust and is served with a honey Dijon mustard sauce.

1 (4- to 5-pound) boneless
  pork loin

1 tablespoon brown sugar

½ tablespoon
  diced garlic

2 teaspoons garlic salt

1 teaspoon freshly
  ground black pepper

2 rosemary sprigs

2 tablespoons
  Dijon mustard

2 tablespoons honey

2 tablespoons cold
  unsalted butter

1 tablespoon chopped
  fresh parsley

1. Preheat the sous vide machine to 137°F.

2. Season the pork loin with the brown sugar, garlic, garlic salt, and pepper. Vacuum seal the pork with the rosemary and drop the bag into the sous vide bath for 2 hours, 30 minutes. When done, carefully remove the bag from the hot water and shock the bag in an ice bath for 2 minutes. Remove the pork from the bag and pat dry.

3. To finish, in a small bowl, mix together the Dijon mustard and honey. Brush one-quarter of the mixture onto the pork and reserve the rest for serving.

4. In a medium cast iron skillet over medium-high heat, melt the butter. Add the pork and sear, including the edges, until brown, about 5 minutes total. Let rest for 5 to 10 minutes before slicing.

5. Plate and serve with the remaining Dijon mustard and honey mixture and a sprinkle of parsley.

PREP TIP   For added flavor, season and vacuum seal the pork a day ahead of cooking.

EASY-PEASY RANCH BONE-IN PORK CHOPS

Serves 4   Prep time: 5 minutes | Cook time: 3 hours | Finishing time: 15 minutes

Here's a shortcut recipe for a quick weeknight dinner. It requires just a few ingredients, including a packet of ranch dressing. It's a reliable meal prep recipe and an easy way to benefit from the convenience of sous vide cooking. When we have a busy week coming up, I make a big batch of mashed potatoes or rice to serve for multiple days with these pork chops. This recipe uses bone-in chops, but boneless pork chops are a great option, too.

2 tablespoons unsalted butter, at room temperature

1 (1-ounce) packet dry ranch dressing mix

½ teaspoon freshly ground black pepper

2 tablespoons finely chopped fresh parsley, divided

4 (1½-inch-thick) boneless pork chops

1 tablespoon olive oil

1. Preheat the sous vide machine to 140°F.

2. In a small mixing bowl, use the back of a fork to mix together the butter, ranch dressing mix, pepper, and 1 tablespoon of parsley to form a paste. Rub the mixture on the pork chops.

3. Vacuum seal the pork chops in a flat layer and drop the bag into the sous vide bath for 3 hours. When done, carefully remove the bag from the hot water and shock the bag in an ice bath for 2 minutes. Remove the pork chops from the bag and pat dry.

4. To finish, in a medium cast iron skillet over medium-high heat, heat the olive oil until it is shimmering. Add the pork chops and sear on each side until a brown crust forms, 30 to 60 seconds. To sear the edges, use tongs to hold the pork chops. Once seared, let the chops rest on a cutting board for 5 to 10 minutes before slicing and serving.

5. Plate with a drizzle of leftover juice from the skillet and the remaining 1 tablespoon of parsley.

BABY BACK RIBS

Serves 4   Prep time: 5 minutes | Cook time: 24 hours | Finishing time: 10 minutes

As a child of the nineties, I remember going to super popular chain restaurants and challenging my brothers to eating baby back ribs. Back then, we aspired to finish off a full rack. These days, my husband and I love baby back ribs because they are sweet and fall-off-the-bone-tender when cooked sous vide style. We like to pick up two racks—one to make that week, and one to freeze and enjoy for a hearty Sunday night dinner. This recipe is pretty true to those ribs I devoured as a kid, except now I have the skills and tools to make them at home. Just as you'd expect at a steakhouse, I like my ribs with thick cut steak fries and coleslaw.

2 racks baby back ribs

1 tablespoon barbecue salt

2 teaspoons freshly ground black pepper

3 tablespoons store-bought barbecue sauce

1. Preheat the sous vide machine to 140°F.

2. Season the ribs with the barbecue salt and pepper. Vacuum seal the ribs in a flat layer and drop the bag into the sous vide bath for 24 hours. When done, carefully remove the bag from the hot water and shock the bag in an ice bath for 2 minutes. Remove the ribs from the bag and pat dry.

3. To finish, preheat the oven broiler to high. Line a baking sheet with parchment paper.

4. Lay the ribs on the prepared baking sheet and broil for 3 to 5 minutes until the barbecue sauce sets, making sure the parchment paper doesn't burn.

5. Plate and serve with mashed potatoes or steak fries.

PREP TIP If you have a smoker, try smoking these with hickory for 1 to 2 hours before sous vide cooking, for additional depth of flavor.

HONEY-CRANBERRY BARBECUE–GLAZED PORK TENDERLOIN

| **Serves 4 to 6** | Prep time: 5 minutes | Cook time: 2 hours, 30 minutes | Finishing time: 20 minutes |

The glaze helps this dish blur the lines between a traditional holiday entrée and a classic summertime dish. It's appropriate for either. In the sous vide bath, the tenderloin is infused with garlic and herb flavors. Once done, it's finished under the broiler with the barbecue glaze. The day after making this pork, if there are any leftovers, I love to dice up what's left and mix it with any remaining barbecue sauce for sweet and savory pulled pork sandwiches. So good!

1 (4- to 5-pound) boneless pork loin

2 teaspoons garlic salt

1 teaspoon freshly ground black pepper

1 rosemary sprig

1 sage sprig

¼ cup Honey-Cranberry Barbecue Sauce (page 152), divided

1 tablespoon chopped fresh parsley

1. Preheat the sous vide machine to 137°F.

2. Season the pork with the garlic salt and pepper. Vacuum seal the pork with the rosemary and sage and drop the bag into the sous vide bath for 2 hours, 30 minutes. When done, carefully remove the bag from the hot water and shock the bag in an ice bath for 2 minutes. Remove the pork from the bag and pat dry.

3. To finish, preheat the oven broiler to high. Line a baking sheet with parchment paper.

4. Lay the pork on the prepared baking sheet and brush the pork with 2 tablespoons of barbecue sauce. Broil for about 5 minutes until browned, making sure the parchment paper doesn't burn. Let rest for 5 to 10 minutes before slicing.

5. Plate and serve with the remaining Honey-Cranberry Barbecue Sauce and a sprinkle of parsley.

SPICY BACON-WRAPPED HOT DOGS

Serves 4   Prep time: 5 minutes | Cook time: 1 hour | Finishing time: 15 minutes

Hot dogs usually come fully cooked when you buy them at the grocery store. So, to most people, sous vide cooking them might be just for fun. But I think the joy in cooking hot dogs this way is that you can wrap them in bacon, making them more flavorful and fun to try. For this recipe, hot dogs are paired with bacon and jalapeño peppers, creating a great option for a cookout or for game day. I mean, why not *sous vide everything you can get your hands on?*

4 hot dogs

4 bacon slices

¼ cup pickled
  jalapeño peppers

4 hot dog buns

Mustard

Ketchup

1. Preheat the sous vide machine to 140°F.

2. Use a fork to poke a few holes in each hot dog. Set aside.

3. On a smooth, flat surface, lay out 1 bacon slice, top it with 4 or 5 slices of pickled jalapeño peppers, lay 1 hot dog on top, then roll to encase the hot dog in the bacon. Repeat for each hot dog.

4. Vacuum seal the hot dogs in a flat layer and drop the bag into the sous vide bath for 1 hour. When done, carefully remove the bag from the hot water, remove the hot dogs from the bag, and pat dry.

5. To finish, preheat the oven to 400°F. Line a baking sheet with parchment paper.

6. Lay the hot dogs on the prepared baking sheet and bake for about 10 minutes until the bacon crisps.

7. Plate and serve with a cold, refreshing beer to calm your mouth from the heat of the jalapeño pepper.

CHAPTER **SEVEN**

find recipe on page 123

BEEF

With sous vide, it's possible to cook any type of steak, exactly how you like it, for only a percentage of the price of eating out. You can also cook amazing steak from frozen (all it takes is an additional hour). Sous vide cooking also gets you a perfect temperature "edge to edge." With steak, this means there won't be a quarter-inch ring of well-done meat around a perfectly medium center. To help this effect, it's important to shock steaks in an ice bath after sous vide cooking so it's easier to sear or grill the outside without affecting the internal temperature of the meat.

Sous vide lets you cook the entire range of beef, from tender and premium steaks to tough and budget-friendly cuts. A crock pot is good for low-and-slow cooking tough cuts such as chuck roasts, ribs, and briskets. A cast iron skillet or grill is ideal for cooking premium cuts of steak, such as New York strips and filets. But you'd never cook a filet in a crock pot or a brisket on the stove in a cast iron skillet.

Unfortunately, many sous vide cookbooks offer a lot of information about cooking the meat but give little information about creating a meal with additional flavors, sauces, and sides. In this chapter, you'll learn how to serve a meal with sous vide beef as the centerpiece. Check the time and temperature chart (page 163) to find the range of times that I have found yields the best results.

BEEF

T-BONE STEAK WITH HERB SAUCE

Serves 4   Prep time: 5 minutes | Cook time: 2 hours, 30 minutes | Finishing time: 20 minutes

Such a handsome cut of meat deserves special treatment. The T-bone cut has both a filet mignon and New York strip in one. Each T-bone is generally big enough to serve two hungry people, maybe three. The herb sauce is a little tangy from the lime with earthy flavors from the cilantro, and the bright-green color is beautiful against the steak.

FOR THE STEAKS

2 (2 pound, 1½-inch-thick)
  T-bone steaks

2 teaspoons salt

1 tablespoon
  diced shallot

10 cilantro sprigs

1 tablespoon olive oil

1½ tablespoons
  diced garlic

4 tablespoons (½ stick)
  cold unsalted butter

FOR THE HERB SAUCE

1 cup roughly chopped
  fresh cilantro

½ teaspoon chili powder

Juice of ½ lime

1 tablespoon olive oil

¼ teaspoon salt

¼ teaspoon freshly
  ground black pepper

TO SOUS VIDE AND FINISH THE STEAKS

1. Preheat the sous vide machine to 130°F.

2. Season the steaks with the salt, then top with the shallots and cilantro.

3. Vacuum seal the steaks in a flat layer and drop the bag into the sous vide bath for 2 hours, 30 minutes. When done, carefully remove the bag from the hot water and shock the bag in an ice bath for 5 minutes. Remove the steak from the bag, discard the herbs, and pat dry.

4. To finish, in a large cast iron skillet over medium-high heat, heat the olive oil until it is shimmering. Add the steak. Add the garlic and butter to the skillet and spoon it over the steak throughout the searing process. Sear the steak on each side for 30 seconds, then sear the edges for 5 seconds each side. Transfer to a cutting board and let cool for 10 minutes before slicing.

5. Plate and serve with the prepared herb sauce.

TO MAKE THE HERB SAUCE

In a food processor, combine the cilantro, chili powder, and lime juice and pulse a few times while pouring in the olive oil. Do not purée, just combine to form a rough texture. Once combined, stir in the salt and pepper.

PREP TIP To cut a T-Bone, first cut off each steak: remove the filet and the New York strip. Then slice each section against the grain.

NEW YORK STRIP STEAK WITH CAROLINA-STYLE YELLOW MUSTARD BARBECUE SAUCE

Serves 4   Prep time: 5 minutes | Cook time: 2 hours, 30 minutes | Finishing time: 15 minutes

It's easy to stock up on New York strips. They are usually sold in warehouse stores and often go on sale at the butcher counter. Being on the bone, they have a ton of flavor, and cooking them sous vide style always results in tender, juicy steaks. In this recipe, the steaks are seasoned simply with garlic salt and pepper. They're served with a tangy Carolina-Style yellow mustard barbecue sauce. It just takes a few minutes to whip up on the stove and tastes great with the steak. I like to make these on the morning of get-togethers and finish them on the grill or sear them in a cast iron skillet when it's time to eat.

4 (1¼-inch-thick) New York strip steaks

3 teaspoons garlic salt

1 teaspoon freshly ground black pepper

1 tablespoon olive oil

1 tablespoon butter

1 tablespoon garlic, diced

2 tablespoons Carolina-Style Yellow Mustard Barbecue Sauce (page 159)

1. Preheat the sous vide machine to 130°F.

2. Season the steaks with the garlic salt and pepper. Vacuum seal the steaks in a flat layer and drop the bag into the sous vide bath for 2 hours, 30 minutes. When done, carefully remove the bag from the hot water and shock the bag in an ice bath for 5 minutes. Remove the steaks from the bag and pat dry.

3. To finish, in a large cast iron skillet over medium-high heat, heat the olive oil until it is shimmering. Add the steaks. Add the butter and garlic to the pan and spoon it over the steaks during the entire searing process. Sear the steaks on each side for 30 seconds, then sear the edges for 5 seconds on each side. Transfer to a cutting board and let cool for 10 minutes before slicing.

4. Plate with a drizzle of barbecue sauce.

BARBECUE SPARE RIBS

Serves 4   Prep time: 5 minutes | Cook time: 24 hours | Finishing time: 15 minutes

This is a regular bulk-prep main dish in my house. I'll buy a large pack of two or four sets of ribs and break them down into smaller portions to sous vide when we're in the mood for ribs. Before freezing, I season them, and I take them out the night before sous vide cooking to thaw. The final step under the broiler gives a slightly chewy exterior to these super-tender ribs.

2 racks spare ribs
(about 20 ribs)

3 tablespoons
barbecue seasoning

1 teaspoon salt

1 teaspoon freshly
ground black pepper

¼ cup store-bought
barbecue sauce

1. Preheat the sous vide machine to 155°F.

2. Season the ribs with the barbecue seasoning, salt, and pepper. Vacuum seal the ribs in a flat layer and drop the bag into the sous vide bath for 24 hours. When done, carefully remove the bag from the hot water and shock the bag in an ice bath for 2 minutes. Remove the ribs from the bag and pat dry.

3. To finish, preheat the oven broiler to high. Line a baking sheet with parchment paper.

4. Lay the ribs on the prepared baking sheet and brush them with the barbecue sauce. Broil for 5 to 10 minutes until the barbecue sauce sets, making sure the parchment paper doesn't burn. Serve hot.

BACON-WRAPPED MEATLOAF

Serves 4 | Prep time: 15 minutes | Cook time: 5 hours | Finishing time: 25 minutes

When something is already good, what do you do to make it even better? Add bacon. So, what could be better than some bacon-wrapped comfort food like meatloaf? Cooking meatloaf in an oven comes with the unfortunate likelihood of it drying out—unless you muddle down the beef flavor with a bunch of additional ingredients. But when you use sous vide, you don't have to be a professional chef to cook a perfectly juicy, beefy meatloaf. The layer of bacon outside the meatloaf produces an extra meaty layer of salty goodness. It's comfort food at its finest.

2 pounds ground beef

2 large eggs

½ cup ketchup

1 tablespoon
  Worcestershire sauce

1 tablespoon diced garlic

½ teaspoon
  onion powder

1 teaspoon dried parsley

½ teaspoon salt

¼ teaspoon freshly
  ground black pepper

1 pound bacon

1 cup tomato sauce

¼ cup freshly grated
  Parmesan cheese

1 tablespoon chopped
  fresh parsley

1. Preheat the sous vide machine to 145°F.

2. In a large mixing bowl, mix together the ground beef, eggs, ketchup, Worcestershire sauce, garlic, onion powder, dried parsley, salt, and pepper until well combined. Set aside.

3. Lay the bacon on a large piece of parchment paper so the pieces slightly overlap. Pour the prepared mixture on the center of the bacon and form a meatloaf log. Use the parchment paper to help fold the bacon around the meatloaf.

4. Vacuum seal the meatloaf (without the parchment paper) and drop the bag into the sous vide bath for 5 hours. When done, carefully remove the bag from the hot water and shock the bag in an ice bath for 5 minutes. Remove the meatloaf from the bag and pat dry.

5. To finish, preheat the oven broiler to high. Line a baking sheet with parchment paper.

6. Lay the meatloaf on the prepared baking sheet and broil for 5 to 10 minutes until the bacon starts to crisp. Let cool for 5 to 10 minutes before slicing into 1½-inch-thick pieces.

7. Plate and serve with the tomato sauce and Parmesan cheese—either on top or as side-condiments—and a sprinkle of parsley.

PREP TIP For the juiciest meatloaf, use 80 percent lean/20 percent fat ground beef instead of leaner options.

LONG-WEEKEND STYLE BURGERS

Serves 4   Prep time: 10 minutes | Cook time: 45 minutes | Finishing time: 10 minutes

There's no need to babysit burgers on the grill when guests are over for a barbecue. Prep these super-juicy burgers the day ahead, sous vide them the morning of the event, and finish them on the grill when it's time to eat. We love to eat our burgers on sweet brioche buns, smeared with a bit of butter and toasted on the grill.

1 pound ground beef

1 teaspoon garlic salt

1 teaspoon freshly ground black pepper

4 burger buns

1. Preheat the sous vide machine to 138°F.

2. In a medium mixing bowl, combine the ground beef, garlic salt, and pepper. Mix well and then divide the burger meat into four 8-ounce patties and flatten into disks.

3. Vacuum seal the burgers in a flat layer and drop the bag into the sous vide bath for 45 minutes. When done, carefully remove the bag from the hot water and shock the bag in an ice bath for 2 minutes. Remove the burgers from the bag and pat dry.

4. To finish, preheat the grill. Grill the burgers on each side until grill marks appear and the outside is browned.

5. Plate with the buns and top as desired.

PREP TIP Serve these with grilled onions. Slice onions a half-inch thick, coat with olive oil, and grill until they soften and grill marks appear.

GUINNESS-BRAISED FILET MIGNON

Serves 4 | Prep time: 5 minutes | Cook time: 1 hour | Finishing time: 10 minutes

The first sous vide dish that I fell in love with was Guinness-braised filet mignon from a little corner restaurant in Baltimore that no longer exists. At the time, sous vide cooking wasn't common, even at restaurants, but this tiny bistro had received a ton of praise in local newspapers for preparing food that way. They served the most tender, melt-in-your-mouth filet. In the fall, I would pair this homey dish with PumpKing beer. In winter, I enjoyed it with a deep-purple Grenache wine. I do wish that restaurant still existed, if only for this dish. In lieu of that, I hope that you enjoy the version I make at home. Freezing the Guinness and broth in cubes before cooking (see the tip) makes it easier to vacuum seal, but if your sealer seals liquids with no problem, or you use the water displacement method (see page 10), you can skip this step.

FOR THE STEAKS

8 ounces Guinness beer, frozen in cubes

4 (6-ounce, 1-inch-thick) filet mignon steaks, or 24 ounces tenderloin tips

1 teaspoon garlic

1 teaspoon salt

¼ teaspoon freshly ground black pepper

8 ounces beef broth, frozen in cubes

1 tablespoon cold unsalted butter

TO SOUS VIDE AND FINISH THE STEAKS

1. Preheat the sous vide machine to 140°F.

2. Season the steaks with the garlic, salt, and pepper. Vacuum seal the steaks in a flat layer with the Guinness and broth cubes and drop the bag into the sous vide bath for 1 hour. When done, carefully remove the bag from the hot water and shock the bag in an ice bath for 5 minutes. Remove the steaks from the bag and pat dry. Retain all juices from the bag for the sauce.

3. To finish, in a cast iron skillet over medium-high heat, melt the butter. Add the steaks and sear until each side is browned with a crust, 1 to 2 minutes.

4. Plate and serve with a drizzle of sauce.

CONTINUED

FOR THE SAUCE

4 tablespoons leftover
beef/beer/stock juice

3 tablespoons cold
unsalted butter

2 teaspoons chopped
fresh thyme

Salt

Freshly ground
black pepper

TO MAKE THE SAUCE

In a small saucepan over medium heat, combine the leftover beef juice (which has the beer and stock in it) and butter. Stir as the liquid reduces to a thick sauce, 5 to 10 minutes. Once it is thick enough to coat the back of a spoon, remove the pan from the heat and add the thyme. Season with salt and pepper.

PREP TIP To freeze the Guinness in cubes, if you choose to do so, in a small saucepan, simmer the beer for a few minutes to burn off the alcohol. Let cool, then pour the beer into an ice cube tray and freeze. For the broth, simply pour it into the ice cube tray and freeze.

GRILLED BEEF KEBABS IN GARLIC-DILL YOGURT

Serves 4   Prep time: 5 minutes | Cook time: 1 hour, 30 minutes | Finishing time: 10 minutes

Sous vide steak kebabs are the ultimate crowd pleaser. The grilled finish allows you to craft this dish to careful precision—bringing the meat to within a few minutes of being done in the sous vide bath, then adding a bit of smoke and crispness on your outdoor grill. If you don't have a grill, a cast iron skillet will work just as well. Tender, juicy, and cooked to a T—these kebabs come together so effortlessly, I feel that I've hardly cooked but still get to serve an all-star meal.

FOR THE KEBABS

1½ pounds sirloin, cut into 3-inch cubes

1 teaspoon garlic salt

½ teaspoon freshly ground black pepper

FOR THE GARLIC-DILL YOGURT MARINADE

½ cup Greek yogurt

1 teaspoon diced garlic

⅛ teaspoon salt

⅛ teaspoon freshly ground black pepper

1 tablespoon finely chopped fresh dill

½ teaspoon smoked paprika

TO SOUS VIDE AND FINISH THE KEBABS

1. Preheat the sous vide machine to 140°F.

2. Season the sirloin with the garlic salt and pepper. Vacuum seal the sirloin in a flat layer and drop the bag into the sous vide bath for 1 hour, 30 minutes. When done, carefully remove the bag from the hot water and shock the bag in an ice bath for 5 minutes. Remove the sirloin from the bag and pat dry.

3. To finish, preheat the grill to high.

4. Skewer the cubes of sirloin and lightly brush the kebabs with the prepared marinade. Grill the kebabs until the marinade burns off and grill marks appear.

5. Plate and serve over rice or a salad.

TO MAKE THE GARLIC-DILL YOGURT MARINADE

In a medium bowl, combine the yogurt, garlic, salt, pepper, dill, and paprika. Mix together until well combined.

PREP TIP If using wooden kebab sticks, soak them in water while the kebabs cook in the sous vide bath. This will prevent burning when on the grill.

FLANK STEAK CHILI LIME TACOS WITH PINEAPPLE GUACAMOLE

Serves 4 Prep time: 5 minutes | Cook time: 1 hour | Finishing time: 10 minutes

Incorporate sous vide cooking into taco night with this recipe. Instead of chewy meat, as you may get from cooking steak traditionally, this recipe results in tender flank steak, cooked evenly and easy to bite into, with all the other taco ingredients.

2 teaspoons diced garlic

1 teaspoon chili powder

1 teaspoon salt

½ teaspoon freshly ground black pepper

1½ pounds flank steak, cut into 2-inch strips (against the grain)

4 cilantro sprigs

½ tablespoon olive oil

FOR THE PINEAPPLE GUACAMOLE

3 large avocados, pitted

2 tablespoons finely chopped fresh cilantro

½ cup crushed pineapples, drained

1 teaspoon diced garlic

⅛ teaspoon salt

1 teaspoon freshly squeezed lime juice

OTHER TACO INGREDIENTS

Tortillas

Rice

Corn

Beans

Sour cream

Tomatoes or salsa

Cotija cheese

TO SOUS VIDE AND FINISH THE STEAK

1. Preheat the sous vide machine to 140°F.

2. In a small mixing bowl, combine the garlic, chili powder, salt, and pepper. Season the flank steak with the prepared rub.

3. Vacuum seal the steak in a flat layer with the cilantro and drop the bag into the sous vide bath for 1 hour. When done, carefully remove the bag from the hot water and shock the bag in an ice bath for 5 minutes. Remove the steak from the bag and pat dry.

4. To finish, in a medium skillet over medium-high heat, heat the olive oil until it is shimmering. Add the steak and sear until browned.

5. Serve DIY style with the pineapple guacamole and other suggested or preferred taco ingredients.

TO MAKE THE PINEAPPLE GUACAMOLE

In a large mixing bowl, use a fork to smash the avocados. Add the cilantro, pineapple, garlic, and salt and combine well. Squeeze lime juice over the top, cover with plastic wrap touching the top of the guacamole (to prevent discoloration), and store in the refrigerator.

READY-TO-PARTY HAWAIIAN MEATBALLS

12 meatballs	Prep time: 20 minutes | Cook time: 1 hour, 30 minutes | Finishing time: 5 minutes

Serve these as an appetizer or make tasty sandwiches with these tangy sweet-and-sour meatballs. When I have the time, I love making big batches of meatballs from scratch. But there's nothing wrong with substituting frozen meatballs for this dish. When cooking from frozen, add 60 minutes to the cook time.

FOR THE MEATBALLS

2 pounds ground beef

2 eggs

½ cup bread crumbs

½ cup chopped
  yellow onion

½ cup chopped
  bell pepper

2 tablespoons
  diced garlic

2 teaspoons salt

2 teaspoons freshly
  ground black pepper

1 tablespoon olive oil

FOR THE PINEAPPLE BARBECUE SAUCE

20 ounces crushed
  pineapples, drained

1 cup store-bought
  barbecue sauce

1 teaspoon diced garlic

TO SOUS VIDE AND FINISH THE MEATBALLS

1. Preheat the sous vide machine to 140°F.

2. In a large mixing bowl, combine the ground beef, eggs, breadcrumbs, onion, bell pepper, garlic, salt and pepper. Mix until well combined.

3. Use a large ice cream scoop to portion out equal meatballs of 2 to 3 inches in diameter.

4. In a large skillet over high heat, heat the olive oil until it is shimmering. Add the meatballs and pan fry until browned to crisp the exterior.

5. Vacuum seal the meatballs in a flat layer and drop the bag into the sous vide bath for 1 hour, 30 minutes. When done, carefully remove the bag from the hot water and shock the bag in an ice bath for 5 minutes. Remove the meatballs from the bag and pat dry.

6. In a large mixing bowl, coat the meatballs with hot barbecue sauce, then plate and enjoy.

TO MAKE THE PINEAPPLE BARBECUE SAUCE

In a medium saucepan over medium heat, mix together the pineapple, barbecue sauce, and garlic and cook for 5 minutes. Remove from the heat and set aside to cool or refrigerate. Reheat before serving with the meatballs.

MOM'S BEST STEW MEAT

Serves 4   Prep time: 5 minutes | Cook time: 24 hours | Finishing time: 10 minutes

This recipe comes from a meal I grew up eating as a kid during the cold winters of Rhode Island. My mom had many shortcuts for cooking, including this one using Catalina dressing as a tangy marinade for beef. She used to slow cook this in the crockpot, and now I make it in a sous vide bath. Mom always served her stew meat with potatoes and carrots, and I do, too. Freezing the dressing in cubes beforehand makes it easier to vacuum seal, but you can always use the water disbursement method (see page 10) instead.

2 tablespoons
diced shallots

1 teaspoon salt

1 teaspoon freshly
ground black pepper

1 cup Catalina dressing,
frozen in cubes

2 pounds beef stew meat

1 tablespoon finely
chopped fresh cilantro

1. Preheat the sous vide machine to 165°F.

2. In a small mixing bowl, combine the diced shallots, salt, pepper, and Catalina dressing. Mix well to combine thoroughly. Add the meat and stir to coat. Pour the contents of the bowl into a bag and assemble in a flat layer.

3. Vacuum seal the bag and drop it into the sous vide bath for 24 hours. Check on the water level throughout the cook to make sure the ingredients remain fully submerged. When done, carefully remove the bag from the hot water.

4. To finish, transfer the contents of the bag to a large saucepan over medium-high heat and cook the stew meat until the remaining liquid dissolves and the beef browns a little bit, about 5 minutes.

5. Plate and serve sprinkled with the cilantro.

SIMPLIFIED BEEF WELLINGTON BITES

Serves 4   Prep time: 15 minutes | Cook time: 1 hour | Finishing time: 35 minutes

This dish will make it look like you went "all-out" to compose a beautiful meal, but the truth is sous vide allows you to take shortcuts. I prefer making these bites to a large Beef Wellington (made with an entire piece of tenderloin) because there's a greater ratio of decadent puff pastry to beef. Smothered between the beef and the pastry is a layer of sautéed mushrooms. The inside of the beef turns out slightly pink, while the pastry puff is a beautiful golden brown.

4 (8-ounce)
  beef tenderloins

2 teaspoons garlic salt

1¼ teaspoons freshly
  ground black
  pepper, divided

2 rosemary sprigs

1 tablespoon olive oil

3 tablespoons cold
  unsalted butter, divided

2 tablespoons
  chopped shallots

¼ cup dry red wine

2 cups chopped
  cremini mushrooms

¼ teaspoon salt

2 teaspoons diced garlic

1 large egg

1 tablespoon water

All-purpose flour,
  for sprinkling

2 sheets puff
  pastry, thawed

1. Preheat the sous vide machine to 135°F.

2. Season the beef tenderloin with the garlic salt and 1 teaspoon of pepper.

3. Vacuum seal the beef tenderloins with the rosemary on top in a flat layer and drop the bag into the sous vide bath for 1 hour. When done, carefully remove the bag from the hot water and shock the bag in an ice bath for 2 minutes. Remove the beef tenderloins from the bag and pat dry.

4. To finish, in a medium skillet over medium heat, combine the olive oil, 2 tablespoons of butter, and the shallots. Cook for 2 to 3 minutes until the shallots begin to brown, then add the red wine. When the wine begins to simmer, add the mushrooms and season with the salt and remaining ¼ teaspoon of pepper. Stir regularly and cook until the mushrooms are coated in wine sauce and the wine dissolves. When done, set aside.

5. In a medium cast iron skillet over medium-high heat, melt the remaining 1 tablespoon of butter. Add the beef tenderloin and sear, then flip and add the garlic. Sear the other side until brown while spooning the butter and garlic mixture over the steak. Once done, let cool a few minutes, then transfer the steaks to a plastic bag and shock them in an ice bath for 2 minutes.

6. Preheat the oven to 400°F. Line a baking sheet with parchment paper.

CONTINUED

7. In a small mixing bowl, beat the egg and water together to create an egg wash.

8. Sprinkle a little flour on a cutting board and roll out the pastry puff sheets a few extra inches. Cut each sheet into quarters.

9. Brush some egg wash onto one puff pastry piece, then place it washed-side down on the prepared baking sheet. Place a steak and then a spoonful of mushrooms on top of the pastry. Brush the edges of the puff pastry with egg wash. Then add a top layer of puff pastry and seal the edges of the dough. Finally, brush the top of the puff pastry with egg wash and use a knife to cut an X in the top. Repeat with the remaining pastry, steak, and mushrooms.

10. Bake for about 15 minutes until golden brown. Remove from the oven and serve hot.

PREP TIP This recipe cooks the beef at a lower temperature of 135°F to account for the time it continues to bake in the oven inside the puff pastry, which will increase the temperature slightly.

SIMPLE SHORT RIBS WITH PEPPERCORN SAUCE

Serves 4 | Prep time: 15 minutes | Cook time: 24 hours | Finishing time: 5 minutes

After experimenting with different cooking durations, I've decided 24-hour short ribs are the way to go. Sure, if you have the patience to wait an extra day or two, let them cook for 36 or 48 hours. But once that shallot-rosemary perfume fills my house, I'm counting down the hours until I can tear open the sous vide bags and dig in! The 24-hour cook time is mostly hands-off and yields perfectly tender, fall-off-the-bone ribs—just like you'd expect at a fine dining restaurant. Serve these tasty ribs over mashed potatoes with the simple peppercorn sauce, and you may never leave home for short ribs again.

FOR THE RIBS

4 tablespoons (½ stick) cold unsalted butter

3 tablespoons olive oil, divided, plus 1 tablespoon more, if needed

2 tablespoons diced shallots

1 teaspoon salt

1 teaspoon freshly ground black pepper

4 pounds short ribs

4 rosemary sprigs

TO SOUS VIDE AND FINISH THE RIBS

1. Preheat the sous vide machine to 180°F.

2. In a small bowl, use a fork to mix together the butter, 2 tablespoons of olive oil, shallots, salt, and pepper to form a paste. Coat the short ribs with the seasoned paste.

3. In a large frying pan over medium-high heat, heat 1 tablespoon of olive oil until it is shimmering. Add the short ribs and sear for 1 to 2 minutes on each side. Add the remaining tablespoon of olive oil if needed to brown all edges of the short ribs.

4. Vacuum seal the seasoned short ribs and rosemary sprigs in two or more bags in a flat layer, leaving a half-inch space between each rib. Drop the bags into the sous vide bath and cover with a lid (if you have one) or aluminum foil. Sous vide for 24 hours, checking the water level and adding more water if needed to keep the bags of ribs fully submerged throughout the cook.

5. When done, carefully remove the bags from the hot water and remove the ribs from the bags. Place them on a plate and cover them with foil to keep them warm. Strain the liquid from the bags over a bowl with a sieve. Alternatively, you can use beef stock to make the sauce.

6. Pour the prepared sauce on the short ribs and serve.

CONTINUED

FOR THE SAUCE

1 tablespoon cold
unsalted butter

½ cup strained juice from
cooked short ribs
(or beef stock)

1 tablespoon
crushed peppercorns

½ teaspoon
Dijon mustard

2 tablespoons heavy
(whipping) cream

¼ teaspoon salt

¼ teaspoon freshly
ground black pepper

TO MAKE THE SAUCE

In a small saucepan over medium heat, melt the butter. Whisk in the strained juice from the cooked short ribs, peppercorns, mustard, heavy cream, salt, and pepper. Stir regularly for about 10 minutes until the sauce turns light brown and is thick enough to coat the back of a spoon.

MAKE IT EASY Leftovers make delicious short rib sandwiches and tacos. Shred the meat before putting it in the refrigerator. Use leftover juice or peppercorn sauce to warm the meat in a pan on medium heat for about 5 minutes.

SPICY BEEF CHUCK

Serves 4   Prep time: 15 minutes | Cook time: 24 hours | Finishing time: 5 minutes

This chuck roast is worth the wait. Typically, tough beef chuck falls apart into tender mouthfuls after the sous vide bath. We eat it in enchiladas for dinner, then in egg scrambles the next day. Regularly check the water level of the sous vide bath to make sure the beef remains submerged during the long cook time. I find that this dish pairs very well with a nice Malbec.

2 teaspoons garlic salt

1 teaspoon freshly ground black pepper

1 teaspoon chipotle powder

3½ pounds beef chuck

2 tablespoons olive oil

1 jalapeño pepper, seeded and diced

1. Preheat the sous vide machine to 140°F.

2. In a small mixing bowl, combine the garlic salt, pepper, and chipotle powder. Rub the beef chuck with the seasonings.

3. In a medium skillet over medium-high heat, heat the olive oil until it is shimmering. Add the beef chuck and sear on each side for 3 to 5 minutes to create a thick brown bark.

4. Vacuum seal the beef chuck with the jalapeño pepper and drop the bag into the sous vide bath for 24 hours. When done, carefully remove the bag from the hot water, remove the beef from the bag, and transfer to a cutting board. With two forks, pull apart the beef until it is well shredded.

5. Serve as desired or freeze for later.

HEARTY SLICED BEEF SANDWICHES

Serves 4   Prep time: 2 hours, 15 minutes | Cook time: 24 hours | Finishing time: 15 minutes

Serve these tender but hearty beef sandwiches for a crowd. In this recipe, you'll sear, sous vide, then sear again to make hearty sous vide beef sandwiches. If you have a smoker, this is a great recipe to smoke for 3 hours before the sous vide bath. Serve these in soft French rolls. To make these sandwiches more Italian style, try swapping mozzarella for the provolone and adding sautéed green bell peppers.

1 (3½-pound) bottom round roast

2 teaspoons chopped garlic

2 teaspoons salt

1 teaspoon freshly ground black pepper

2 tablespoons olive oil, divided

1 rosemary sprig

¼ cup red wine

2 tablespoons cold unsalted butter

4 (8-inch) French rolls

4 tablespoons mayonnaise

1 cup sautéed onions (optional)

8 slices provolone cheese

1. Preheat the sous vide machine to 140°F.

2. Rub the beef with the garlic, salt, and pepper.

3. In a skillet over medium-high heat, heat 1 tablespoon of the olive oil until it is shimmering. Add the beef and sear it on each side for 3 to 5 minutes to create a thick brown bark. Remove the beef and add the rosemary, wine, and butter to the skillet. Deglaze the skillet, scraping up any brown bits, until the liquid reduces by half. Remove the rosemary, then strain the jus through a sieve into a bowl. Pour the jus into an ice cube tray and freeze for 2 hours.

4. Vacuum seal the beef with the wine jus and drop the bag into the sous vide bath for 24 hours. When done, remove the beef, reserving the liquid.

5. Turn a skillet to medium-high heat, heat 1 tablespoon of the olive oil until it is shimmering and add the cooked beef. Sear beef on each side for 3 to 5 minutes for the final sear. Transfer it to a cutting board and let it rest for 5 minutes before slicing it thinly for sandwiches.

6. To finish, in a small saucepan over medium heat, simmer the reserved beef juice, butter, and leftover wine sauce from the previous day for 5 minutes. Transfer the sauce to individual bowls for dipping, if desired.

7. To assemble the sandwiches, smear 1 tablespoon of mayonnaise on the base of each roll, drizzle with a spoonful of wine sauce, then add a few slices of beef, sautéed onions (if using), and 2 slices of provolone.

SMOKY SOUS VIDE BRISKET

Serves 4   Prep time: 10 minutes | Cook time: 48 hours | Finishing time: 5 minutes

For this recipe, use either a smoker for 3 hours or a grill for a quick sear to infuse flavor into the brisket before the sous vide bath. When it's done, the meat turns out tender and ready for a slather of barbecue sauce. This meat is perfect for barbecue brisket sandwiches or quesadillas.

2 teaspoons smoked salt

1 teaspoon freshly ground black pepper

1 teaspoon ground cumin

1 (3-pound) beef brisket

2 tablespoons olive oil

1. Preheat the sous vide machine to 135°F.

2. In a small mixing bowl, combine the smoked salt, pepper, and cumin. Rub the brisket with the mixture.

3. In a large cast iron skillet over medium-high heat, heat the olive oil until it is shimmering. Add the brisket and sear on each side for 3 to 5 minutes to create a thick, brown bark.

4. Vacuum seal the brisket and drop the bag into the sous vide bath for 48 hours. When done, carefully remove the bag from the hot water, remove the brisket, and transfer to a cutting board. Pull apart the beef with two forks or cut it for sliced brisket.

PREP TIP With a long cook like this one, check the water level and make sure the beef remains fully submerged throughout the cook.

MOJO SAUCE–MARINATED FLANKEN RIBS

Serves 4 | Prep time: 5 minutes | Cook time: 48 hours | Finishing time: 10 minutes

Flanken ribs are thin ribs cut across the bone. One day, years ago, we brought them home not knowing what they were but determined to figure them out. Quickly, we found that the sous vide bath transforms this typically chewy cut of meat into soft, tender bites of beef. The mojo sauce is a perfect herby complement to the ribs. Use it as a marinade during the sous vide bath, then as a finishing sauce for extra flavor.

1 teaspoon salt

½ teaspoon freshly ground black pepper

1¼ cups Mojo Sauce (page 158), divided

3 pounds flanken-style ribs (also called Hawaiian- or Korean-style ribs)

1. Preheat the sous vide machine to 145°F.

2. In a small mixing bowl, combine the salt, pepper, and ¼ cup of mojo sauce. Season the flanken ribs with the mixture.

3. Vacuum seal the ribs in a flat layer and drop the bag into the sous vide bath for 48 hours. When done, carefully remove the bag from the hot water, remove the ribs from the bag, and pat dry.

4. To finish, preheat the grill to high.

5. Grill the flanken ribs until grill marks appear on each side. Plate and serve with extra mojo sauce.

HONEY-GARLIC TRI-TIP STEAK

Serves 4   Prep time: 5 minutes | Cook time: 2 hours | Finishing time: 15 minutes

Sweet, salty, and a little bit sticky, this tri-tip hits all the notes. Serve with brown rice, stir-fried vegetables, or sautéed broccoli. Any leftovers make tasty steak salads the next day.

1 tablespoon chopped garlic

¼ teaspoon red pepper flakes

1 teaspoon salt

½ teaspoon freshly ground black pepper

3 pounds tri-tip steak

1 tablespoon olive oil

⅔ cup Honey-Garlic Sauce (page 144)

1. Preheat the sous vide machine to 130°F.

2. In a small mixing bowl, combine the garlic, red pepper flakes, salt, and pepper and mix thoroughly. Season the steak with the mixture.

3. Vacuum seal the tri-tip in a flat layer and drop the bag into the sous vide bath for 2 hours. When done, carefully remove the bag from the hot water. Remove the tri-tip from the bag and pat dry.

4. To finish, in a large cast iron skillet over medium-high heat, heat the olive oil until it is shimmering. Add the tri-tip and sear for 30 to 60 seconds, then flip the tri-tip and add 3 tablespoons of the Honey-Garlic Sauce. Spoon the sauce over the tri-tip while the other side cooks. Remove from the heat when a brown crust has formed on all sides, including the edges.

5. Transfer the tri-tip to a cutting board and let rest for 10 minutes before slicing. Plate and pour any leftover sauce, as desired, on top. Extra sauce can go on any rice or vegetables that you might serve with the dish.

JERK STEAK BOWLS

Serves 4 Prep time: 5 minutes | Cook time: 1 hour | Finishing time: 20 minutes

Skirt steak flavored with jerk seasoning makes these rice bowls something to crave. Substitute cauliflower rice to go lighter or add the jerk steak and toppings to lettuce to make salads. Serve with your favorite accompaniments.

2 pounds skirt steak

1 tablespoon diced shallots

2 tablespoons Jerk Seasoning (page 147)

3 cilantro sprigs

½ tablespoon olive oil

3 cups cooked preferred rice (or cauliflower rice), **divided**

2 avocados, pitted and diced

1 cup diced tomatoes

1 cup cooked corn

TOPPING IDEAS

Sour cream

Chopped fresh cilantro

Lime wedges

Hot sauce

Cheddar cheese

Crumbled tortilla chips

1. Preheat the sous vide machine to 140°F.

2. Season the skirt steak with the shallots and jerk seasoning. Vacuum seal the skirt steak in a flat layer with the cilantro on top and drop the bag into the sous vide bath for 1 hour. When the skirt steak is done, carefully remove the bag from the hot water, remove the steak from the bag, and pat dry.

3. To finish, in a medium cast iron skillet over medium-high heat, heat the olive oil until it is shimming. Add the steak and sear until browned, 30 to 60 seconds on each side. Let rest for 10 minutes before cutting.

4. Layer the ingredients in four jerk steak bowls beginning with one-quarter of the rice and continuing with one-quarter of the steak, avocados, tomatoes, corn, and whichever additional toppings you desire.

find recipe on page 118

EIGHT

find recipe on page 152

SPICE RUBS, SAUCES, AND MARINADES

This chapter has a plethora of ways to season your sous vide dishes and turn them into meals. It's a smart idea to make extra sauces and dressings for specific recipes, then save the extras to use as marinades for future dishes. Many of these ideas can be stored, either in a dry pantry, in the refrigerator, or in the freezer, ready to use at a moment's notice.

Sauces and marinades can be a little tricky to use with sous vide, depending on your vacuum sealer or technique. One way to get around this is to freeze the liquids in an ice cube tray. Then when you're ready to sous vide, pop out a flavor-packed cube and vacuum seal it with your food. It will thaw in the sous vide bath and add a ton of flavor to the dish.

Most of the sauces in this chapter are safe to refrigerate and use for up to 3 days. If you plan to use them after that time, I suggest freezing them in ice cube trays, as mentioned.

SPICE RUBS, SAUCES, AND MARINADES

HONEY-GARLIC SAUCE

About ⅔ cup   Prep time: 10 minutes | Cook time: 10 minutes

Enjoy this on any protein—wings, chicken, fish, and pork are great choices. It's a thick sweet-and-sour sauce that has a zing from the fresh ginger and garlic. Use it as a dip or marinade as you'd like.

1 teaspoon olive oil

1 tablespoon cold
  unsalted butter

1 tablespoon diced garlic

⅓ cup honey

1 teaspoon freshly
  grated ginger

2 tablespoons
  brown sugar

2 tablespoons soy sauce

¼ teaspoon red
  pepper flakes

1. In a small saucepan over medium heat, combine the olive oil, butter, and garlic. Sauté for 1 to 2 minutes, stirring regularly so the garlic doesn't brown.

2. Once the garlic becomes translucent, add the honey, ginger, brown sugar, soy sauce, and red pepper flakes.

3. Raise the heat to medium-high to bring the sauce to a boil, then reduce the heat to medium-low and simmer for about 5 minutes until the sauce easily coats the back of a spoon.

LEMON-HONEY-PEPPER GLAZE

About ½ cup Prep time: 5 minutes | Cook time: 10 minutes

This thick, sweet-but-peppery glaze is insanely delicious on chicken and fish. It's perfect for brushing on protein right before it's seared in a pan or broiled in the oven.

¼ cup apple
  cider vinegar

⅓ cup honey

½ cup stock
  (chicken or vegetable)

2 teaspoons freshly
  ground black pepper

1 teaspoon freshly grated
  lemon zest

1 tablespoon freshly
  squeezed lemon juice

¼ cup olive oil

In a small saucepan over medium-low heat, combine the vinegar, honey, stock, pepper, lemon zest, lemon juice, and olive oil. Cook, whisking regularly, for 5 to 10 minutes until the glaze ingredients integrate.

SWEET SESAME-GINGER DRESSING

About ⅓ cup   Prep time: 10 minutes | Cook time: 10 minutes

This sweet-and-savory dressing pairs well with chopped fresh scallions and a sprinkle of sesame seeds.

1 tablespoon sesame oil

2 tablespoons diced garlic

1 teaspoon fresh ginger, grated

1 tablespoon soy sauce

1 tablespoon rice wine

Juice of ½ lime

1. In a small saucepan over medium heat, combine the sesame oil and garlic. Sauté for 1 minute, stirring, until the garlic becomes translucent.

2. Add the ginger, soy sauce, rice wine, and lime juice and continue to cook, stirring, for 2 minutes.

3. Reduce the heat to medium-low and simmer for about 3 minutes until the mixture reduces and becomes a thick dressing.

JERK SEASONING

This is a tasty seasoning to sprinkle on everything from chicken to shrimp to pork.

2 teaspoons allspice

2 tablespoons
  brown sugar

½ teaspoon
  ground cumin

¼ teaspoon
  onion powder

¼ teaspoon dried parsley

¼ teaspoon
  ground cinnamon

¼ teaspoon
  ground nutmeg

⅛ teaspoon
  cayenne pepper

1 teaspoon garlic salt

½ teaspoon freshly
  ground black pepper

In a medium mixing bowl, combine the allspice, brown sugar, cumin, onion powder, parsley, cinnamon, nutmeg, cayenne pepper, salt, and black pepper.

LEMON-TAHINI SAUCE

About ⅔ cup Prep time: 10 minutes

It's creamy, lemony, and so addictive! The herbs are bright and fresh, and the lemon really stands out, making this a great sauce for fish and chicken.

½ cup tahini paste

1 tablespoon diced garlic

1 tablespoon diced shallot

2 tablespoons freshly squeezed lemon juice

1 tablespoon chopped fresh dill

1 tablespoon chopped fresh parsley

In a bowl, combine the tahini, garlic, shallot, lemon juice, dill, and parsley and mix well. Chill in the refrigerator until ready to serve.

GARLIC-DILL BUTTER

About ¾ cup   Prep time: 10 minutes

This garlic dill butter can be enjoyed on so many dishes, both sous vide and beyond. It's a beautiful butter to serve for holidays, too. Make it in large batches and have it on hand to smear on fresh bread.

½ cup (1 stick) unsalted butter, melted

2 tablespoons olive oil

1 tablespoon chopped fresh dill

1 tablespoon chopped fresh garlic

Salt

Freshly ground black pepper

1. In a medium mixing bowl, combine the butter, olive oil, dill, and garlic. Season with salt and pepper and mix until well combined.

2. Spoon the butter onto plastic wrap and form into a 2-inch-thick log. Roll in the wrap and chill in the refrigerator.

OLIVE BUTTER

About ¾ cup   Prep time: 10 minutes

This olive butter is salty and complex. Totally unexpected. And perfect on any protein or Mediterranean dish.

½ cup (1 stick) unsalted butter, melted

¼ cup Kalamata olives, pitted and diced

1 tablespoon diced garlic

1 teaspoon salt

1. In a medium mixing bowl, combine the butter, olives, garlic, and salt and mix together well.

2. Spoon the butter onto plastic wrap and form a 2-inch-thick log. Roll in the wrap and chill in the refrigerator.

BLUE CHEESE SLAW

Okay, so not technically a sauce, but this slaw is definitely a condiment type of dish you have to try. Use this tasty slaw to top any burger, wrap or sandwich. It lasts 2 to 3 days in the refrigerator.

1 cup shredded carrots

½ cup diced red onion

¼ cup blue
  cheese dressing

2 tablespoons finely
  chopped fresh cilantro

In a large mixing bowl, combine the carrots, onion, dressing, and cilantro and mix well. Refrigerate until serving.

HONEY-CRANBERRY BARBECUE SAUCE

About 2 cups   Prep time: 5 minutes | Cook time: 20 minutes

Is it barbecue sauce? Is it cranberry sauce? Well, it's both, which makes it a great condiment to enjoy year round. Generously pour this sweet and sour barbecue sauce on poultry, pork, meatballs, or steak dishes. It has a beautiful deep purple hue and looks great with chopped green herbs.

1 cup cranberries, fresh
  or frozen

½ cup honey

1 tablespoon brown sugar

¼ cup ketchup

¼ cup red wine vinegar

1 tablespoon freshly
  squeezed lemon juice

½ teaspoon garlic salt

½ teaspoon
  onion powder

¼ teaspoon freshly
  ground black pepper

1 tablespoon
  Worcestershire sauce

In a medium saucepan over medium heat, combine the cranberries, honey, brown sugar, ketchup, vinegar, lemon juice, garlic salt, onion powder, pepper, and Worcestershire sauce. Bring the mixture to a gentle boil, then reduce the heat to medium-low and simmer for 15 minutes until the sauce is thick enough to coat the back of a spoon.

CREAMY CHIPOTLE SAUCE

About ½ cup   Prep time: 10 minutes

Drizzle this creamy, spicy sauce on proteins and seafood. It's also great on top of burgers with avocado.

¾ cup heavy
(whipping) cream

2 teaspoons puréed
chipotle in adobo sauce

Juice of ½ lime

1 tablespoon finely
chopped fresh cilantro

Salt

Freshly ground
black pepper

1. In a small saucepan over medium-low heat, heat the heavy cream, stirring regularly, for 2 to 3 minutes.

2. When the cream has reduced by half, whisk in the chipotle and turn off the heat.

3. Whisk in the lime juice and cilantro. Season with salt and pepper to taste. Chill in the refrigerator.

SWEET HONEY-SRIRACHA SAUCE

About 1 cup   Prep time: 10 minutes

The perfect sweet-and-spicy companion is my go-to for fish, shrimp, poultry, and green beans. There's no reason to use Sriracha sauce straight out of the bottle when you can turn it into a super interesting, balanced sauce.

4 tablespoons honey

4 tablespoons soy sauce

3 tablespoons lime juice

5 teaspoons Sriracha sauce

4 teaspoons rice vinegar

½ teaspoon red pepper flakes

3 tablespoons minced garlic

1 tablespoon sesame seeds (optional)

3 scallions, diced (optional)

In a large mixing bowl, mix together the honey, soy sauce, lime juice, Sriracha sauce, rice vinegar, red pepper flakes, and garlic. If desired, use sesame seeds and scallions as garnishes.

POMEGRANATE GLAZE

About ⅔ cup　Prep time: 10 minutes

This sweet glaze is phenomenal on poultry and pork dishes. It tastes great on crispy chicken skin broiled in the oven and looks so pretty drizzled on top of food.

½ cup pomegranate molasses

1 tablespoon apple cider vinegar

2 tablespoons honey

½ teaspoon salt

¼ teaspoon freshly ground black pepper

In a medium mixing bowl, whisk together the pomegranate molasses, apple cider vinegar, honey, salt, and pepper until well combined.

SESAME SAUCE

About 1½ cups   Prep time: 10 minutes | Cook time: 20 minutes

While this sauce is a classic for chicken and fish, it really pairs well with veggies, especially green beans and carrots.

½ cup sugar

2 tablespoons cornstarch

¾ cup water

2 tablespoons
rice vinegar

1 tablespoon soy sauce

1 tablespoon sesame oil

½ teaspoon red
pepper flakes

1 teaspoon diced garlic

1 teaspoon diced
fresh ginger

1 tablespoon
sesame seeds

1. In a small saucepan over medium heat, whisk together the sugar, cornstarch, and water until the sugar and cornstarch dissolve.

2. Add the rice vinegar, soy sauce, sesame oil, red pepper flakes, garlic, and ginger, and stir regularly until the mixture comes to a boil.

3. Reduce the heat to medium-low and simmer for 10 minutes. Use sesame seeds as a garnish.

SOY-SRIRACHA SAUCE

About 1 cup Prep time: 10 minutes

*Another one of my favorite uses for Sriracha sauce, this recipe is super simple.
Throw a piece of fish, steak, or chicken in a dish to caramelize in the sauce, and
your dinner guests will be impressed.*

½ cup soy sauce

2 tablespoons Sriracha

2 teaspoons honey

1 tablespoon brown sugar

¼ teaspoon red
  pepper flakes

In a bowl, whisk together the soy sauce, Sriracha,
honey, brown sugar, and red pepper flakes.

MOJO SAUCE

About 1½ cups   Prep time: 10 minutes

This is the traditional sauce used to marinate Cuban sandwiches, but it tastes great on a variety of proteins. Make it in large batches to use as a marinade. Brush it on proteins before grilling or searing. Or freeze it in ice cube trays and pop a cube or two in a sous vide bag before vacuum sealing it with protein.

3 tablespoons
  diced garlic

4 tablespoons freshly
  squeezed lime juice

4 tablespoons freshly
  squeezed orange juice

¼ cup olive oil

½ teaspoon finely
  chopped fresh oregano

¼ teaspoon
  ground cumin

1 teaspoon salt

In a medium mixing bowl, combine the garlic, lime juice, orange juice, olive oil, oregano, cumin, and salt and mix together well.

CAROLINA-STYLE YELLOW MUSTARD BARBECUE SAUCE

About 1 cup   Prep time: 5 minutes | Cook time: 20 minutes

This sauce has just the right amount of sweetness and tang, and you'll be surprised at how easily it whips up from scratch. Sometimes called Carolina barbecue sauce, it's a perfect pairing for those summer meat dishes.

2 tablespoons
  unsalted butter

½ cup yellow mustard

¼ cup brown sugar

1 tablespoon honey

¼ cup apple
  cider vinegar

2 tablespoons water

1 teaspoon chili powder

1 teaspoon
  ground chipotle

¼ teaspoon freshly
  ground black pepper

¼ teaspoon
  onion powder

¼ teaspoon garlic salt

In a small saucepan over medium heat, melt the butter. Add the mustard and stir to combine. Reduce the heat to medium-low and add the brown sugar, honey, vinegar, water, chili powder, chipotle, pepper, onion powder, and garlic salt. Simmer, stirring regularly, for 15 minutes.

HOLLANDAISE SAUCE

About 1½ cups | Prep time: 5 minutes | Cook time: 10 minutes | Finishing time: 5 minutes

Not just for eggs, hollandaise sauce is a creamy, rich egg-and-butter sauce that makes dishes from breakfast to dinner more indulgent. It requires setting up a double broiler, which is a pot filled halfway with water, with a mixing bowl placed on top. In the double boiler is where the eggs, butter, and lemon juice are whisked together. Add this thick, rich sauce to poached eggs, proteins, and vegetables.

6 egg yolks

¾ cup (1½ sticks) unsalted butter, melted

2 tablespoons freshly squeezed lemon juice

½ tablespoon chopped fresh parsley, for serving

1. Create a double boiler by filling a large cooking pot halfway with water and placing a mixing bowl on top of the pot, so the base sits inside the pot but doesn't touch the water. Bring the water to a gentle simmer over medium-high heat.

2. In a mixing bowl, combine the egg yolks and lemon juice and whisk together so the yolks form small bubbles. The extra air helps aerate the hollandaise sauce, producing a very light sauce.

3. Pour the egg yolk mixture into the double boiler bowl and slowly add the melted butter, whisking the mixture the entire time while the butter integrates with the mixture. Do not stop whisking the eggs: They will overcook if left to sit in the bowl.

4. Within moments, the sauce will become thick enough to coat the back of a spoon. As soon it reaches this stage, take the pan off the heat. Continue to whisk the sauce regularly until you're ready to serve. For a final touch, sprinkle the parsley on top of the sauce once the sauce is added to your food.

COOKING TIMES AND TEMPERATURES

This book outlines cooking temperatures and times based on personal preference. The information here will provide more detail on the ranges of doneness and cooking times (both minimum and maximum times) to help you build your own recipes. These ranges show the minimum times that certain foods need to be cooked in order to be safe to eat. You will also see that some foods can cook for longer than the recipes in this book state, giving you some flexibility in timing.

BEEF

Steaks (tender cuts) should be cooked at least 1 hour and typically no more than 3 hours.

> RARE: 129°F/54°C—1 to 2 hours
> MEDIUM: 136°F/58°C—1 to 2 hours
> WELL DONE: 154°F/68°C—1 to 2 hours

Roasts (prime rib, rib roast) should be cooked longer to help break down connective tissue, between 5 and 16 hours.

> RARE: 133°F/56°C—5 to 16 hours
> MEDIUM: 140°F/60°C—6 to 12 hours
> WELL DONE: 158°F/70°C—5 to 10 hours

Tough Cuts (brisket, chuck roasts, eye of round) need to be cooked at least 8 hours and up to 48 hours.

> RARE: 131°F/55°C—24 to 48 hours
> MEDIUM: 149°F/65°C—20 to 24 hours
> WELL DONE: 185°F/85°C—8 to 16 hours

PORK

Chops (loins) should be cooked at least 1 hour and typically no more than 3 hours.

RARE: 136°F/58°C—1 to 3 hours
MEDIUM: 144°F/62°C—1 to 3 hours
WELL DONE: 158°F/70°C—1 to 3 hours

Roasts (prime roasts) should be cooked longer to help break down connective tissue, between 3 and 6 hours.

RARE: 136°F/58°C—3 to 6 hours
MEDIUM: 144°F/62°C—3 to 4 hours
WELL DONE: 158°F/70°C—3 to 3 hours, 30 minutes

Tough Cuts (belly, shoulder) need to be cooked at least 8 hours and up to 24 hours.

RARE: 140°F/60°C—8 to 24 hours
MEDIUM: 154°F/68°C—8 to 24 hours
WELL DONE: 185°F/85°C—8 to 16 hours

CHICKEN

Light Meat (breasts) should be cooked at least 1 hour and no more than 3 hours.

SOFT AND JUICY: 140°F/60°C—1 to 3 hours
TENDER AND JUICY: 149°F/65°C—1 to 3 hours
WELL DONE: 167°F/75°C—1 to 3 hours

Dark Meat (legs, thighs) should be cooked at least 1 hour and no more than 5 hours.

TENDER AND JUICY: 149°F/65°C—1 to 5 hours
FALL OFF BONE: 167°F/75°C—1 to 5 hours

FISH

All fillets should be cooked for at least 45 minutes and no more than 1 hour, 15 minutes.

TENDER AND SOFT: 104°F/40°C—45 minutes to 1 hour, 15 minutes
TENDER AND FLAKY: 122°F/50°C—45 minutes to 1 hour, 15 minutes
WELL DONE: 131°F/55°C—45 minutes to 1 hour, 15 minutes

VEGETABLES

Green vegetables differ from root vegetables and cooking times can range from 10 minutes to 3 hours, but all temperatures remain the same.

GREEN VEGETABLES: 185°F/85°C—10 to 20 minutes
GOURDS: 185°F/85°C—1 to 3 hours
ROOT VEGETABLES AND POTATOES: 185°F/85°C—2 to 3 hours

MEASUREMENT CONVERSIONS

	US STANDARD	US STANDARD (OUNCES)	METRIC (APPROXIMATE)
VOLUME EQUIVALENTS (LIQUID)	2 tablespoons	1 fl. oz.	30 mL
	¼ cup	2 fl. oz.	60 mL
	½ cup	4 fl. oz.	120 mL
	1 cup	8 fl. oz.	240 mL
	1½ cups	12 fl. oz.	355 mL
	2 cups or 1 pint	16 fl. oz.	475 mL
	4 cups or 1 quart	32 fl. oz.	1 L
	1 gallon	128 fl. oz.	4 L
VOLUME EQUIVALENTS (DRY)	⅛ teaspoon		0.5 mL
	¼ teaspoon		1 mL
	½ teaspoon		2 mL
	¾ teaspoon		4 mL
	1 teaspoon		5 mL
	1 tablespoon		15 mL
	¼ cup		59 mL
	⅓ cup		79 mL
	½ cup		118 mL
	⅔ cup		156 mL
	¾ cup		177 mL
	1 cup		235 mL
	2 cups or 1 pint		475 mL
	3 cups		700 mL
	4 cups or 1 quart		1 L
	½ gallon		2 L
	1 gallon		4 L
WEIGHT EQUIVALENTS	½ ounce		15 g
	1 ounce		30 g
	2 ounces		60 g
	4 ounces		115 g
	8 ounces		225 g
	12 ounces		340 g
	16 ounces or 1 pound		455 g

	FAHRENHEIT (F)	CELSIUS (C) (APPROXIMATE)
OVEN TEMPERATURES	250°F	120°C
	300°F	150°C
	325°F	180°C
	375°F	190°C
	400°F	200°C
	425°F	220°C
	450°F	230°C

RESOURCES

anovaculinary.com: Anova has a bunch of ideas for using sous vide machines to their fullest. From user guides to recipes, there are many ideas on the site to get the creative juices flowing. These days, I have most of the times and temps memorized for my taste, but when I was starting out, using this site was helpful to make sure I was cooking recipes to the best specs.

chefsteps.com: This site has beautifully laid out information and guides for sous vide cooking.

cooksillustrated.com: This is another thorough site. I love their egg charts and shrimp charts that show dozens of options for different cook times and what the food will look like at different intervals.

sipbitego.com: Sip Bite Go has tons of step-by-step sous vide recipes with videos and photos of cooking sous vide meals. There are plating suggestions, wine pairing ideas, and different finishing options for a variety of proteins, vegetables, and more.

sousvidemagazine.com: This site has a ton of stuff for newbie sous vide enthusiasts to dig into, from historical information about this cooking method to restaurant-inspired recipes.

INDEX

ACKNOWLEDGMENTS

Thanks for inviting me into your kitchen. I'm so happy to have shared my sous vide recipes with home cooks like you. Trust yourself and dive in to all the flavor ahead!

It's been a journey to get here, from experimenting with my first Easy Bake Oven as a kid to working in restaurants while going to art and business schools to meeting the love of my life, Patrick, who just happened to be a chef. While the creativity was always there, my culinary skills really propelled forward with his support and encouragement in the kitchen.

I'm grateful for everyone—and there have been many people—who have been a part of my journey from conception to launch of Sip Bite Go. It takes a lot of guts to build and launch something from scratch, plus an army of people to support the vision. Pivoting from a 9-to-5 job to pursue my passions wasn't easy, and it definitely wasn't a straight line from A to B. I'm very thankful for everyone who believed I could make the leap as I explored my path to becoming a creative entrepreneur.

Special thanks to the entire publishing team who helped bring this book to life. Michael and Aric, your humor and expertise was much appreciated as we tackled each chapter. It's not easy to wrangle a rogue blog writer who dodged as many English classes as possible, but you did it, and I'm so proud of the results. High five.

ABOUT THE AUTHOR

Jenna Passaro is a food and travel writer, photographer, and sous vide enthusiast based in Portland, Oregon. She is the creator of *SipBiteGo.com*, which shares recipes and travel guides for foodies. Jenna and her husband, Patrick, are world travelers who met while he was a chef in Baltimore. Since then, they moved across the country, had a wedding that included llamas, and, most recently, had a baby. As new parents, they are on a mission to balance life with eating delicious meals at home, and want to help others do the same. Jenna's work has been featured on *Southern Living*, KGW Portland, Bing, and Yahoo, among others.

CPSIA information can be obtained
at www.ICGtesting.com
Printed in the USA
BVHW021342281221
625053BV00019B/926